LIFT

★ ★ ★

A BUSINESS FABLE FOR TEAMS AND THE PEOPLE WHO LEAD THEM

DALLAS BURNETT

FREILING
AGENCY

Published by Freiling Agency, LLC.

P.O. Box 1264
Warrenton, VA 20188

www.FreilingAgency.com

PB ISBN: 979-8-9888007-7-4
HB ISBN: 979-8-9888007-6-7
eBook ISBN: 979-8-9888007-9-8

Printed in the United States of America

Dedication

To my trio of inspirations, Eva, Ellis, and Everli.

Contents

Acknowledgments

What an adventure! My writing comes from my experiences and helps me make sense of the world. This book was no different and has helped me refine my view on teams and organizational culture.

First, thank you to the Freiling Agency and for believing in this concept from the beginning. Also, specifically, thank you to Tom for the hours and hours you spent with me hammering out this project. Thank you for not giving up on it and helping make this project come to life. I am grateful.

To my incredible wife: You've journeyed through these pages with me, long before they were bound into a book. Thank you for giving critical feedback at a pivotal time in the process. Without her encouragement, support, and insights, this book would not be possible.

A huge shout out to the amazing team at Palmetto. We've lived many of the concepts of this book together. Your willingness to adapt, to enhance our shared culture, and to drive the company's spirit forward has been transformative. I especially want to thank Kiel Bradley for seeing the vision and whole-heartedly embracing what it means to go from a performer to a leader/coach. Your dedication and growth are inspiring to see. Thank you for sitting through some very long sessions on Monday mornings while we worked through so many ideas that are now in this book!

Finally, thank you to my daughters Eva, Ellis, and Everli for always caring about how my day goes and laughing with me and Danielle over dinner. Your energy, passion for life, and kind spirits make the days very sweet and the journey more exciting.

Preface

My books come from my work and life experience; this project was no different. After releasing *MOVE!* I found myself leading a company that needed a big cultural shake-up. I didn't create the original culture. I hadn't hired everyone, and the technical side of things wasn't remotely close to my expertise. Even still, I was responsible for shifting the culture from toxic to healthy, from territorial to collaborative, from change-resistant to growth-oriented, and from a me-first approach to a we-first mission-minded organization. This wasn't a quick fix; it was a marathon of over four years, and the work continues. The company set performance records every year of my tenure, but I am more proud of the records they continue to set after my departure. Great leaders develop great companies, but great cultures develop great leaders. They're nailing it, and I can't wait to see where they head next.

Now, the million-dollar question: How did we do it? It wasn't a one-man show. Some key leaders were committed to this transformation, and the organization became more consistent in living its values. We drove home the idea to our leaders (who were very male and very technical) that even though work is full of transactions, our goal was higher. If we lead teams, the transactions should be the results, dashboards, deliverables, or reports. However, many times, we were transactional with the people we led. Leading needed to be more than numbers. It's about people, their growth, and rising to meet their potential. It's about transformation. We have to care. We have to be open about what we know and don't know. Becoming a transformational leader takes much more work, honesty, and effort. How do you take something old and make something new? Transformation.

During my time at the company, we revamped their leadership summits. We created great spaces for people to ask hard questions, be challenged, grow, and be inspired. We would always provide a book for the summit participants based on the topic or theme of the year. However, most people did not enjoy reading leadership books. They would do it, but it was half-hearted except when the book was in the form of a story. When they read stories, the entire dynamic of the discussion changed. People were engaged, shared more, and even commented on how much they enjoyed the book. So I decided my next book would be a business fable.

The strategies and levers that we employed to overhaul our company culture? They're all in here. This book isn't just about metrics or processes. This is about the heart of any business—the people. It's about turning individuals into a team, a team into leaders, and an organization into a powerhouse. We're tackling the big question: "How do we truly change and strengthen the culture of a team or organization?" Dive in, and let's find out together. Ready? Let's jump into the story!

SECTION 1

Scott's Dilemma

"A true leader creates a
culture in which dedication
and hard work feel like a
natural choice rather than
an obligation."

1

Scott Gets a New Job

Nestled under a busy airplane route, Scott's office building often shook with the sounds of jet engines, interrupting his thoughts with their loud roars. This would annoy most people, but not Scott. Instead, the noise motivated him. Scott worked in a management position at an aviation supply company. He'd been fascinated by air flight since he was a kid, and the sight of planes descending gracefully for a landing always amazed him. Some of these big planes weighed more than 100,000 pounds, but they landed as gently as a feather. Watching this daily show from his office window became an important ritual for Scott, a constant reminder of why he was grateful for his job.

When he took this job, which was a step up from his previous position, Scott had high hopes of a bright future. He was a rising star in the industry. He was recruited and hired by the company's owner, Dave Ettinger, who was practically a legend in the aviation community and the kind of guy people wanted to work for. Dave possessed a unique quality that naturally inspired dedication and hard work among his employees. His approachability and genuine interest in each individual's success created an environment of mutual respect and trust. Everyone went the extra mile for Dave!

But reality turned out to be different from what Scott expected. The problem was that Dave wasn't around much anymore. When Scott joined the company, Dave's presence loomed large. Little by little, however, he left his responsibilities to a senior manager, Gary Domintello, whose leadership could be intense. His management style was characterized by a high degree of control, and as a result, the environment became increasingly stifling. Suggestions and input from team members were overshadowed by Gary's firm direction, and Scott was having a hard time dealing with the manager's demands. The sense of being part of a team had gone missing.

In his last job, Scott thrived in a strong culture where everyone worked well together. He enjoyed his work because of the positive energy and teamwork. When he was hired and then promoted to this new management role, he was confident in his ability to lead a team. He looked forward to bringing people together and achieving progress under Dave's guidance. However, in his absence, Scott and his co-workers felt increasingly disconnected. The company's operations and revenue were taking a real hit. But Scott kept pushing ahead despite the challenges, and he tried to make up for it with his strong work ethic.

Scott often asked himself what made Dave such a great guy to work for and how he became so successful as a team builder and leader. What were the qualities that made Dave stand out, creating a culture in which dedication and hard work felt like natural choices rather than obligations? How did he make his employees feel motivated to contribute their best efforts? These questions became Scott's constant companions, but he wasn't finding many answers. Meanwhile, the turbulence was taking its toll on Scott's morale.

Another Day at the Office

Up in the sky, another airplane drew lines in its path, catching Scott's attention for a moment. But his thoughts were rudely interrupted by Gary, whose words always hit Scott like wind shear, snapping him out of his thoughts: "Hey, Scott, I need your weekly report. Please get it to me by the end of the day. I'm tired of the excuses." He was terse, as usual. Scott quickly apologized, tried to be polite, and agreed to

Gary's demand. Gary's penchant for reports was a thorn in Scott's side, and it took precious time away from spending quality time with his team.

In some ways, Gary reminded Scott of a younger version of himself. He was a driven, high-energy manager, the type of guy who looked as if he graduated at the top of his business school. Gary was determined and he had big expectations, so people in the office took him seriously, probably too seriously. The staff was mostly afraid of Gary, so employees found ways to avoid him, which led to a general sense of avoidance company-wide. Scott often buried himself in his laptop when Gary was around because he didn't want to talk to him. His laptop became like a shield that he used to hide from Gary and from his co-workers. It's partly what led to Scott's own feelings of disengagement. This disengagement was not only a detachment from the task at hand; it was also a slow erosion of his potential.

One morning, Scott took a quick trip to the coffee pot and spotted a co-worker named Emily. She was a trusted friend in the office. As they sipped their coffee together, she said, "You know, Scott, I've been sensing a real lack of team spirit around here lately. It feels like we're all working in our own bubbles. It's stressing me out."

Scott nodded in agreement, appreciating Emily's openness. "You're right, Emily," he sighed. "We're all focused on our individual tasks, but there's a missing sense of team. It's been bothering me, too."

Then Gary wandered in. Their conversation suddenly stopped, and Scott and Emily politely went their separate ways. Scott was still stressed out but glad to know he wasn't the only one feeling the pressure. Meanwhile, he was handed a Key Performance Indicators (KPI) report on the way into his office. He was so dismayed by how bad the numbers looked that he crumpled up the report and threw it into the wastepaper basket.

This wasn't how Scott used to be. When he came on board with the company, he was full of energy and ready to face each day's challenges with excitement. Now his thoughts had become more negative, affecting not just his work but also his personal life. While he hadn't completely given up on himself or his work, he'd developed an attitude that was affecting everyone around him. He was constantly running from one meeting to another, sending emails, jumping on Zoom calls, and managing countless text messages. It was as if everything held the same priority and he'd become the proverbial mouse on a wheel!

Each week, Scott held a staff meeting. Sometimes Dave would drop by and join in the team's conversation, offering his perspective and encouraging them all. But that wasn't happening anymore, and the weekly meetings weren't going so well. The meetings were crucial because they set the tone for the team. They were also where they problem-solved getting airplane parts to their customers. Pilots relied on Scott's team to keep their planes in the air, and when the team was unable to deliver a part on time, the company lost money and customers.

Scott was peppered with questions during his meetings. Amy always talked about problems with customers who weren't receiving the correct parts. She asked Scott repeatedly, "What should we do about these complaints?"

At this point Scott was exasperated and resorted to answering, "Tell them to be patient and wait; we'll send them the missing parts soon. Anything else?"

Amy seemed perturbed. Then another person on the team, Tony, talked about someone getting promoted and suggested that they have lunch to celebrate. Tony asked Scott, "Can we treat Ted to lunch? What do you think?"

Scott agreed but also suggested he was too busy to join in on the fun. "Yeah, sure, Tony. I'm really busy this week and next, so have fun."

More questions kept coming: *When are our budgets due? When are we going to see the new database? What do we do with Gary's latest email?* As the meeting continued, the questions became more serious and Scott's answers less helpful. He did his best to answer questions but often kicked the can down the road. He didn't ask the team for much feedback, either. He sat quietly and doodled on a piece of paper, wondering about his next move.

Scott's team found itself in a vicious circle. With goals vaguely defined, the team began to drift aimlessly. The absence of a clear, unifying direction led to confusion taking root. The team members' ideas collided, and they routinely forgot which tasks were most important.

As motivation waned, collaboration faltered, and a general sense of frustration continued to increase.

The whole thing began to feel like the movie *Groundhog Day*. This is when and where Dave's presence would have really helped!

Scott Goes Home

After the meeting, Scott took a long drive home, seeking a brief escape from his thoughts. When he eventually arrived, his tired wife met his gaze, reflecting her concern. "Was your day okay?" she asked, her voice carrying some worry.

Scott, weighed down by mixed feelings, responded with a low murmur before heading to the kitchen. He was thinking about what would make a day "good," but he couldn't find a satisfying answer. He wanted some time alone to untangle the complicated thoughts in his mind.

Sarah's watchful eyes followed his every move. He sat down at the dining room table without saying anything. She stood nearby, looking both determined and worried. "Scott, we need to talk," she said. "You're a rock star at work and you always have been. What's going on?"

He avoided eye contact, focusing on his dinner instead. She asked again, but he didn't answer.

The truth was, Scott felt stuck, as if he were on autopilot with no clear direction, and he didn't know how to land the plane.

Scott and Sarah moved to the couch where he finally opened up a bit. "You know, Sarah, these past few weeks have been really tough," Scott sighed, his voice tinged with exhaustion. "It feels like nothing I do is making a difference with the team. Then there's Gary, always pushing and never acknowledging the effort we're putting in. And Dave, well, we hardly see him anymore."

Sarah looked at him with empathy, placing a reassuring hand on his. "I can only imagine how overwhelming it must feel," she responded gently. "But you've faced tough situations before, Scott. Remember when you led that project last year? It seemed impossible at first, but you pulled through and exceeded everyone's expectations."

Scott looked at Sarah, finding comfort in her words. "Yeah, you're right. I did manage to turn things around back then," he acknowledged.

His face brightened a bit, a glimmer of hope breaking through his uncertainty. Sarah squeezed his hand. "And I have no doubt that you'll get through this and come out stronger on the other side. Who knows—maybe you'll meet someone who will help you out."

As Scott absorbed her words, he felt some renewed determination. Maybe his challenges were opportunities in disguise.

"A great CEO fosters an atmosphere of camaraderie and genuine rapport with everyone around them."

2

Scott's World Turns Upside Down

The following morning, Scott stepped back into the office, his stomach gripped by familiar knots of anxiety. Along with his usual tasks for the day, an additional weight bore down on him: he must present a report to Gary detailing the concerning dip in his team's productivity and the unexpected over-stepping of his budget. A double-whammy.

He contemplated blaming factors beyond his control, hoping to divert Gary's scrutiny. The idea of seeking his team's insight also briefly flitted through his mind, but the potential dissent would be uncomfortable. So he knew he must face Gary alone as a one-man-show. Avoidance became his prevailing strategy—a response to the challenges that swamped him. When he failed to unite his team's efforts, he always fell back to taking the helm single-handedly, pulling along those under his charge. So he would grind it out and give Gary the answers he needed.

Before diving into his work, Scott walked down the hallway and passed the coffee pot. An unusual sight captured his attention: his co-workers congregating in the glass-walled conference room. The gathering puzzled him, as he was unaware of any scheduled meetings. Uncertainty gnawed at him, fueled by the fear of missing communication about a meeting. He noticed that other colleagues were similarly abandoning their desks and gravitating toward the conference room. Intrigued, he followed the tide of people.

Upon Scott's arrival at the conference room, a sea of stunned expressions greeted him, bewilderment and surprise etched on each face. Murmurs of disbelief circulated, accompanied by disapproving headshakes. His curiosity piqued, Scott positioned himself to eavesdrop, attentively leaning in, but then Gary made his entrance, causing the room to go silent.

Gary's body language told the tale; his typically composed demeanor was disrupted by unexpected news that clearly caught even him off guard. "Ladies and gentlemen, I want to confirm that our worst fears have come true. Dave passed away last evening," he plainly stated, his voice conveying a mixture of surprise and somberness.

They all knew Dave had been sick, but nobody had any idea that he might not live long. The atmosphere in the room became a combination of astonishment and a concealed grief, as the impact of this news reverberated through everyone. The emotions became palpable, prompting both men and women to tears. Dave was much more than a proprietor and CEO; he was a cherished friend whose presence would be dearly missed.

"Dave's absence will be deeply felt," Scott quietly interjected, his words carrying a blend of respect and sorrow. Among his team, many nodded their heads, affirmed his sentiment; additional voices also echoed their feelings. Their sorrow created an unspoken bond, reminding them of the impact Dave had on their lives and the void his departure left behind.

Gary's voice sliced through the stillness. "Let's reconvene to our tasks, everyone. I'll disseminate further information as it becomes available." His words signaled a call to action, yet as the attendees filtered out of the room, a peculiar shift occurred. Instead of heading back to their cubicles, they gravitated to each other, forming small clusters. The directive to resume work was unheeded, overshadowed by the need to process thoughts and feelings.

Dave Ettinger's legacy loomed large, his founding of the company four decades before that day serving as a testament to his visionary leadership. Under his stewardship, the modest aviation supplier flourished into a regional juggernaut, earning acclaim as the leading company of its kind. He was the archetypal CEO, embodying a rare combination of intellect and diligence, while fostering an atmosphere of camaraderie. His affable nature and genuine rapport with everyone garnered him universal affection. But now, Dave was gone.

From Uncertain to Uncertainty

Some days you get out of bed and nothing special or unexpected happens. You feel as if you're in control. Other days you get out of bed and your world turns upside down. This was one of those days.

Dave had interviewed and hired Scott. In fact, he recruited him, "wined and dined" him, and persuaded him to come on board with an attractive offer. Dave was the reason Scott left his previous employer. So his death really shattered his world. Scott had been recruited like an NCAA all-star by the best coach in the league. Now the coach was gone and this all-star felt as if he were left holding the ball. Now what?

He decided to go to his car and call his wife. "Sarah, you won't believe this, but Dave died."

She was silent for more than a moment, and then tried to encourage him. "I'm sorry. That's terrible news." She paused again. "Look, Scott, things happen for a reason. We've always said that to each other. So try to keep your cool today, and we'll talk about it tonight."

Scott paused as well and didn't say anything.

"Scott, are you listening? Take it easy, and we'll talk this evening."

He agreed, slid his phone into his back pocket, took a few moments to gather his thoughts, and walked back into the office.

It was hard to focus the rest of the day. Scott reached out to his team and asked them to meet later that afternoon. They ran through the usual routine, but it was hard for everyone to focus. "Scott, Dave's presence is really going to be missed around here. I'm nervous. What's next?" asked his most senior team member.

"I'm not sure. I think at this point, we all just need to be patient and keep doing our work. We'll find out more soon," was all Scott could think of to say. He'd never experienced a loss of leadership like this, and he was unsure of his own thoughts, much less how to move his team through it. He agreed that Dave's loss would cause a vacuum. Uncertainty would soon pervade the workplace. "Let's all meet again tomorrow, guys." Scott got up and walked out of the room.

That evening when Scott got home, Sarah met him at the door with a hug. They walked back out the door together and headed to their favorite restaurant. She did her best to encourage him. "We don't always know what to expect when we get up in the morning, Scott. But we have to believe that good will come of this," she said quietly but firmly.

"I don't see it, Sarah, but I'll try not to panic."

Scott didn't get much sleep that night.

Another Unexpected Twist

As dawn broke the following day and Scott walked back into the office, sat down, and opened his laptop, his attention was instantly drawn to an email: an invitation to a noon meeting with the senior managers of the company. Amidst his daily tasks, he couldn't help but think about this upcoming meeting in a similar light to an impending dental appointment—a blend of necessity and apprehension. But he thought the meeting at least might be an opportunity for some clarity and direction.

Guided by Gary's authoritative presence, the meeting began. As the room settled into attention, Gary candidly began to outline the transition, but only after sharing a few memorable stories about Dave. He explained that the long-term future of the company was uncertain. Then, amidst his unfolding narrative, the air was thick with anticipation when Gary pulled out a letter from his jacket pocket. "Dave penned a letter," he said while holding a piece of paper in the air, "and he asked the Board to follow its instructions." Scott was tense while Gary began to read it. Gary cleared his throat and read aloud:

Dear Valued Team,

I hope this letter finds you all in good health and spirits. I cannot even begin to express my gratitude to each of you as I reflect upon the remarkable path our company has traversed over the past four decades. But change is an inevitable constant in both life and business.

With that in mind, I want to share my vision for the company's future. I am entrusting the helm of our company to Gary, who will serve as our acting CEO. Gary understands our industry backwards and forwards and has been with us for many years.

I've had the pleasure of observing and working with Scott Turner, one of our newest managers. His dedication, commitment, and unwavering drive have not only caught my attention but also secured my confidence in his abilities to carry forth the values and ethos that have defined us. So I'm placing Scott second-in-command as our COO.

Gary and Scott's journey ahead will not be without its trials, but their integrity, leadership, and determination will undoubtedly steer us through any storm that may come our way. I am confident that they will continue to develop the culture we've nurtured together, one that champions teamwork, respect, and excellence.

Remember that our collective strength is what has made us successful, and it is this unity that will propel us forward under Gary and Scott's capable leadership. I have the utmost faith in their ability to not only lead but also to inspire each of you to continue striving for greatness. I wholeheartedly believe that the best days of the company are still ahead of us, and I am excited to witness it from above.

Thank you for your unwavering dedication, loyalty, and hard work. Each of you has shaped this company into what it is today. Let's continue to support one another and rally around Gary and Scott as they usher in this new era.

With heartfelt gratitude and best wishes for the future,

Dave Ettinger
Founder and Former CEO

An undercurrent of astonishment passed through the room, rendering Scott, Gary, and everyone assembled in a state of disbelief. Scott, whose reputation wasn't particularly distinguished yet, found himself grappling with the stark contrast between his self-perception and the perspective held by Dave. An eerie silence settled over the room as Gary extended an invitation for Scott to join him at the head of the conference table. Their hands met in a firm shake, the weight of the moment palpable.

With all eyes on him, Scott was offered the platform to say a few words. However, he was so blindsided by the turn of events that his ability to articulate was diminished. He displayed a nervous smile as he searched for words, the unexpected situation temporarily leaving him at a loss. He said nothing, smiled, and sat down.

Gary appeared disappointed as he said, "Well, let's all get back, everyone, and please feel free to see me privately if you have questions." The meeting broke, and one by one, people streamed out of the conference room, with a few shaking Scott's hand or patting him on the back. He thought he heard someone mumble the word "shocker," but he wasn't sure.

Amidst the dynamic shifts in the corporate landscape, Scott now found himself facing an unexpected twist in his career. As if in a scene straight out of a whirlwind, he was suddenly handed the reins to a much larger team—an entire company, in fact. This unforeseen promotion propelled him into the spotlight, a role he once aspired to, but he now felt a mixture of both excitement and unease. The weight of this new responsibility pressed heavily on his shoulders. Leading a new team, steering the destiny of an entire workforce, was a daunting endeavor, one that left him with an internal conflict between self-doubt and the desire to prove himself.

The next day he would meet with his new team, a larger team, the *entire* team. He felt empowered, but of course, he was nervous as well. He wasn't sure what to expect from them, what he should even say, and how she should deal with the potential fallout. He needed some fresh air, so he stepped outside and walked a gravel path around the airfield, not more than ten minutes away. He wouldn't be missed for long.

"Restoration begins with

identifying problems."

3

Scott Meets Ray

Adjacent to Scott's office building was a regional airport that was devoid of extensive security measures, which provided him the liberty to amble close to the runway. Engulfed in a cloud of introspection, he was poised for the next aircraft's passage above.

As his anticipation heightened, Scott caught a glimpse of a small aircraft positioned near the far end of the runway. An unfamiliar sight, this small plane piqued his curiosity, prompting him to draw nearer. Could there be an upcoming air show? Did the plane crash? He moved toward it.

The vintage airplane, a biplane, stood as a testament to a bygone era, its aged exterior hinting at a long retirement harkening to aviation's golden years. The image of an "airplane graveyard" crossed Scott's mind, drawing parallels with the remnants of history. A pair of weathered seats cradled memories, a broken propeller spoke to the craft's once-thriving life, though one was marked with wear. Two wings arched above the weathered frame, and a set of deflated tires accentuated the aircraft's grounded existence. No discernible brand emblems graced its exterior, but the fuselage bore the word "Boomerang," which he assumed was the airplane's name.

Suddenly, a presence caught him off guard—a seasoned and very bearded man emerged from the cockpit. Scott's heart raced, not only because of the unforeseen company but also due to the peculiar appearance of this newcomer. The old man's laughter echoed, his lanky frame gracefully descending from the cockpit, his outstretched hand a gesture of camaraderie. "Nice to meet you, aviator," he greeted. Scott found himself taken aback by the scenario. Now seated nonchalantly on the plane's wing, the old man's aviator goggles rested atop his forehead, his gaze directed toward the heavens.

Scott was surprised by what he said next.

"Need a lift?" the old man inquired, a glint of camaraderie in his eyes.

Scott chuckled and responded, "Well, it seems this vintage plane isn't quite ready to spread its wings anytime soon."

A warm smile graced the old man's lips as he assured him, "Oh, there's no rush. Today definitely isn't the day for a flight. There are old pilots and bold pilots, but never old, bold pilots!" They both laughed. "The name's Ray, and what's yours?"

Scott promptly replied, "I'm Scott."

Ray was affable with a welcoming presence. "Pleasure to meet you, Scott. Feel free to drop by anytime. This bird may seem weathered now, but she was once a trophy. I'm set on restoring her former glory. Restoration begins with identifying problems, and trust me, we've got our share with this old plane. Yet, with some patience, skill, and a touch of grace, we'll revive her and take to the skies. I'd be glad for some company."

Engaged in more conversation, Scott realized that Ray really knew his stuff as far as airplanes go. As their chat wound down, Scott expressed his need to return to the office. With a hearty pat on the shoulder, Ray bid him farewell. "See you soon, Scott. You'll be back, right?"

"Why, certainly," Scott replied. He sensed that Ray was looking forward to meeting again soon.

As Scott walked back to his workspace, the old man's words resonated in his thoughts, particularly when Ray said, "Restoration begins with identifying problems," because Scott knew he had more than a few problems ahead of him. And there was something about Ray that left a lasting impression. It was a connection that Scott sensed would draw him back again soon. Meanwhile, back to his "team."

Scott Goes to Work

Back at the office, Gary asked to meet with Scott again. Scott's intuition told him that Gary harbored a veiled animosity toward him. Subtle cues in their interactions, the undertones in their conversations, and the guarded glances exchanged during meetings led Scott to believe that Gary might be nursing a hidden grudge. The way Gary's demeanor seemed to subtly shift whenever Scott discussed his ideas or achievements fueled the suspicion that Gary might secretly relish the prospect of Scott stumbling. While he had no concrete evidence to support this sentiment, Scott's gut feeling cast a shadow of doubt over their working relationship.

It was a long meeting, and Gary did most of the talking. Scott listened attentively and took copious notes. As the meeting progressed, the tension increased. Team-building or fostering collaboration were not mentioned Gary's agenda. Instead, their discussion gravitated toward meticulous details, KPIs, and the minutiae of daily operations. Gary's authoritative approach dominated the discussion.

As the meeting progressed, it became evident that his focus was firmly fixed on the intricacies of tasks and performance metrics, leaving no space for team dynamics and rapport-building that Scott remembered from Dave. Gary was nothing like Dave in this way, Scott thought to himself.

As the meeting concluded near the end of the day, Scott was exhausted and he needed to escape Gary's stifling personality, so he swiftly made his way toward the exit. Returning to the scene of his newfound friend and his vintage airplane, Scott approached Ray.

"I'm surprised you're back so soon, Scott!" Ray exclaimed, his demeanor once again warm and inviting.

Scott's response echoed his sentiment: "I needed some fresh air."

Ray's intentions for the late afternoon unfolded as he described his plan to disassemble the engine. "Why don't you stick around and watch?" he asked. The invitation was extended with generosity. "Grab a chair and I'll show you a thing or two."

Settling into a weathered lawn chair, Scott assumed his place as an eager observer. Ray went back to work on the plane. Their conversation took flight, spanning about two hours, as Scott delved into all that happened at work. He unloaded as Ray tended to the engine, listening intently to Scott's narrative and offering the gift of his unwavering attention.

Meanwhile, Ray's old and worn hands deftly worked on the intricate process of disassembling his airplane engine. With a keen eye for detail, he began by methodically removing the weathered outer casing, exposing the heart of the engine. Gears, their teeth worn smooth by years of revolutions, were delicately coaxed free, and Ray's fingers navigated the network of valves and pistons, carefully dislodging each piece. As the engine's interior was unveiled layer by layer, Scott was impressed with how well Ray understood the inner workings of an airplane engine.

While continuing to watch, Scott told Ray about his problem. He admitted, "My problem, Ray, is that frankly I'm afraid to lead this new team. I really don't have any idea what I'm doing. I'm working hard, but apparently I'm hardly working."

Ray chuckled. "Don't we know it, Scott—you're flying in the clouds upside down!" Scott knew that a pilot can become confused in the clouds, and Ray was correct in his assessment. His analogy wove a thread between his vintage airplanes and Scott's challenges in building a team.

"It sounds like we have some work to do, Scott. You're a lot like this old airplane I'm restoring. It doesn't look like much today, but with a little work, she'll fly like a bird once again," Ray said with a smile. "When *Boomerang* crashed, I wasn't injured too badly, but it was a setback, and of course I couldn't fly her any longer. So I quit flying planes until I got my head together. It really threw me for a loop and I was afraid to fly again, so I went into business for myself and opened a small airplane engine parts company. It wasn't much of a company, but I needed a break, and it paid the bills. I learned a lot, though, starting and running a business. It sounds like you and I have a lot in common, Scott. We both survived a crash landing and aren't sure what to do about it."

Scott looked at Ray and nodded. Somehow he felt a strong camaraderie with Ray, and he appreciated his candor. He looked at his watch and realized he had to get back to the office. So he got up out of his chair and leaned in to shake Ray's hand. "I'll drop by again tomorrow, Ray."

As he turned and walked away, Ray said, "Don't you worry, Scott. We all need a little lift now and then!" Scott smiled and walked back to the office with a little more pep in his step.

"You rise when you raise others. You can't do it all alone."

4

Scott's First Team Meeting

Gary called again for another long meeting and a demand that Scott hold long meetings of his own with his team to fix the company's mounting problems.

Their relationship was now showing visible cracks as the pressure increased. Scott couldn't shake the feeling that Gary was homing in on his vulnerabilities, like a predator sensing his prey's weakness. Every interaction felt like a minefield, with Scott convinced that Gary was orchestrating a strategy to engineer his downfall. The weight has left Scott with more self-doubt and caused his mental game to go off the rails. He talked himself "up" daily, but nonetheless, he increasingly felt there was no way to win.

That evening, Scott peppered his wife with questions. She was no freshman when it came to business either; before they had children, she was the office manager at a busy law firm. "Sarah, if you were in my shoes, how would you start the meeting tomorrow?

Should I ask the staff members to introduce themselves? Do I jump right into tasks? Should I ask for each person's advice? Should I schedule follow-up meetings with team members? Give them individual goals?" His list went on. But Sarah hadn't had much team-building experience herself. She encouraged Scott with kind words but no sage advice. He was happy nonetheless for that. He turned in early to try for a good night's sleep.

As Scott walked into the conference room the next morning, he found the whole team gathered and looking at him. He was holding a coffee mug and had a laptop and tablet with him. He tried to seem friendly, but a bit of nervousness was hidden behind his smile. As he sat down, everyone's eyes were on him, waiting for him to start. He had carefully planned what to say, but he still felt the pressure. He looked at his tablet for a moment, took a breath, and began.

During the meeting, Scott talked a lot about the numbers, as Gary demanded, but his attempt to impress fell short because his presentation of the data was confusing. When people asked questions, he avoided answering directly. When someone challenged his data, he responded by trying to control the situation instead of asking for more feedback, which just made the numbers more confusing. As the meeting went on, Scott talked a lot, but his words didn't clarify anything. He talked in circles, sometimes even answering his own questions. Even though he was acting as if he knew what he was doing, the team looked puzzled. He kept going, saying that he would send emails with to-do tasks, but that promise went unfulfilled as the day became busier and more chaotic. The unfinished to-do lists made everything even more confusing.

"Scott, there's so much information coming at us. How are we supposed to remember everything?" The nodding around the room reinforced their bewilderment, revealing that Scott's data overload had left the team even more confused. Scott paused, momentarily taken aback by the question, realizing he was getting nowhere.

With each passing hour of the meeting, the weight of responsibility crushed Scott's resolve. The chaos seemed to mount. It eventually ended, mostly because he and the entire team were too exhausted to go on. He moved back to his desk, which had become a triage station for the steady stream of team members asking questions. He madly dialed vendors and suppliers in a desperate bid to keep everything afloat.

Meanwhile, the cycle of long, ineffective meetings continued, exacerbated by Scott's inability to delegate. His notes and to-do lists multiplied, his calendar bursting with obligations. He began comparing himself to a professional juggler, working on reports for Gary while on video calls with suppliers and vendors. He tried to keep the team motivated between all his meetings and calls while remaining calm through it all, but Scott wasn't sure about the next steps he should take with his team members.

It was another rough week.

Time to Find Ray

Friday afternoon, Scott diverted his attention from emails and text messages. Binoculars in hand, he trained his gaze on the horizon where Ray's vintage airplane sat. After viewing the distant activity for a few moments, he decided to abandon his desk and venture outside. It was another stifling South Carolina summer day, thick with heat and humidity. He stepped out into the dust-laden wind and made his way to see Ray.

Spotting Ray beneath the airplane's underbelly, Scott leaned over and greeted him with a smile. "Hey there, Ray. How's the progress coming?"

Ray's familiar voice resonated, "Scott! I've been wondering when you'd come by." Emerging from beneath the plane, he dusted off his hands and stood upright. "Tea time, my friend. Take a load off." Retrieving bottles from a cooler, Ray extended one to Scott in a gesture of hospitality, and they settled into their seats.

Ray's eyes fixed on Scott as he took a deep breath, "Ray, I'm pouring in the hours, pushing myself to the limit, but there's something missing. Still, I'm trying to keep my own spirits up."

Ray's looked up to the clouds, lost in thought. After a reflective pause, he again focused on Scott, his words carrying the weight of experience. "Scott, remember this crucial truth: you rise when you raise others. You can't do it all alone. It's time to roll up our sleeves. There's work to be done, my friend."

"Your predicament,
your challenge, is that you're
leading but you're yet
to be a true leader."

5

Ray Talks About Teams and Teamwork

Ray launched into a monologue on the art of teamwork. To Scott's surprise, the old airplane mechanic with a big burly beard revealed wisdom well beyond his appearance. Ray's discourse unfolded with such rapid-fire momentum that Scott found himself taken aback.

After a brief pause, Ray inquired, "Do you have more time on your hands, Scott?"

Scott hesitated for a moment and then responded, "Sure, maybe an hour or so."

With a nod, Ray grabbed two weathered green lawn chairs that were sheltered under a tree. "Take a seat, Scott." They settled into their chairs, and Ray commenced.

"Your demeanor tells a story, Scott," Ray began. "You are self-assured, driven by ambition and energy, and a real expert in your field. And I can sense you're not one to shy away from pushing your limits. Am I right?"

The accuracy of the assessment surprised Scott. Ray had good intuition! The thought crossed his mind, *We've only recently met, yet Ray seems to have me pegged down to the finest detail.* "Absolutely, that's spot on," Scott replied.

Ray's gaze narrowed slightly as he leaned in, "So, Scott, tell me about your team."

Some names rolled off Scott's tongue, each member summoned to life through his descriptions: "Bill, Todd, Gwen, Lisa, Shannon, Jackson, Shirley, Brianna, Hernandez, Bailey, Crystal, Peter—those are my managers. Of course, there are many others." He talked about their roles, their personalities, and how they've mostly been underperforming.

During this exchange, Scott didn't hold back his concern about the rather lackluster state of his team meetings. "Ray, I'm I'm sensing resistance, or maybe my instructions fall on deaf ears. Either way I can't help but feel some strain in our dynamic. They're not fully on board with my leadership."

Ray, unperturbed, encouraged Scott to be honest with himself and with others: "It sounds like you're personally carrying most of the burden, Scott. You're going it alone because you can't get your team to go with you.

"Allow me to share a tale, not of airplanes, but of geese," Ray continued, guiding the conversation into a new terrain. He recalled a goose's near miss with his airplane. "Geese fly together in formation. You grasp the idea of flying in formation, right?"

After Scott's agreement, Ray went on with the story. "Imagine this—you're covering thousands of miles during migration, and energy conservation is paramount. If you constantly flap your wings, exhausting your strength, you won't get too far." A knowing look exchanged between them as Ray's arms mimicked the motion of wings flapping, a symbol of the lesson about to unfold.

"But when these geese collaborate as a cohesive unit, their collective energy increases significantly. When they organize into a V-formation, each bird is strategically positioned, providing a windbreak for the one ahead. This arrangement, a calculated alignment both above and beside each other, exploits not only the reduction of wind resistance but also the updraft created by the lead goose's movement." Ray's hands gracefully illustrated his words. "They synchronize their flaps, move together, and rotate roles. The lead goose, breaking the wind, eventually falls back to allow another to take the lead, bene-fiting from the updraft."

Scott absorbed these words, reflecting on their implications for leadership and team-building. Ray's voice draws him back. "Did that sink in, Scott? They flap together, and they fly together, taking turns." Scott contemplated these insights as Ray continued. "Your predicament, YOUR challenge, Scott, is that you're perpetually at the tip of that V-formation. You're in perpetual flight, incessantly flapping. Flap, flap, flap." Ray enacted the motion again, a bird-like gesture with his arms. "And then you wonder why fatigue sets in and your team seems to lag behind. You're leading, Scott, but you're yet to be the true leader."

Those words penetrated deeply. Ray's perspec-tive was a revelation of sorts. Scott's commitment and hard work had never been questioned. It was his approach that was under scrutiny. Dave recog-nized Scott's dedication when he hired him, but the relentless striving appeared to be reaching its limit. The metaphor of the geese hit home—his frenetic wing flapping wasn't yielding the desired outcomes. He envisioned himself flying solo soon, the rest of the flock unable to keep up. For the first time, the significance dawned on him—he must evolve from

merely "leading by doing" into a leader who empowered the team to achieve.

"So how can I transform, Ray? How can I truly
become an effective leader and change the culture of
my team?" The urgency and uncertainty in Scott's
tone reflected his genuine need for guidance.

Ray offered a tangible solution. "Tomorrow's the
start, Scott. A fresh day, a fresh perspective. School
begins tomorrow. Come by early Saturday morning,
and over some fried eggs, we'll chart the course."
With a firm handshake and a nod of his head, Scott
departed, an air of anticipation surrounding the
beginning of a new chapter.

On the journey back to the office, Scott's gaze
lingered on the distant figure of Ray, his arms
mimicking geese in their V-formation. A sense of
eagerness filled him, the anticipation of both break-
fast and the transformative conversation that lay
ahead.

SECTION 2

Reminders

"Being a leader is more than just working hard or sharing information. It's about setting a direction."

6

Ray Reminds Scott

On Saturday morning, there was a soft breeze and the temperature was a warm 72 degrees. It was a perfect day to relax by the runway, watch planes come and go, and listen to Ray talk about working together as a team. Scott was the first one up at home. He made a big cup of coffee and headed to the airport. He sent a quick text to his wife, letting her know he was leaving early, which was unusual because he usually slept in. He was in good spirits.

Ray was busy working on his airplane as usual when Scott dropped by. The plane's pieces were now all spread out on the ground, organized but not messy. When Scott approached, he started the conversation: "Hey, Ray, looks like you're making great progress on getting the plane back in the sky!"

"Well, Scott, there's still a lot to do. After taking it apart, I have to decide which parts to keep and which to throw away. It's a job, for sure, but I'm excited to see her again. And speaking of jobs, being a pilot is the only one that comes with an office in the sky!" Ray's answer, accompanied by a grin, sounded adventurous.

Later, sitting in their lawn chairs, Ray began talking again about building a strong team. "Scott, the key to a good team is reminding them regularly what's most important. Reminders are the foundation of team leadership. And that's your job; you are the Chief Reminder Officer. Never assume things; every important message needs to be confirmed. Reminders make sure everyone is on the same page, working toward the same goals."

Ray explained that part of Scott's challenge as a leader was that his team might sometimes be confused about what's important and what's not as important. Scott's rapid-fire approach (instilled by Gary, nonetheless) might be leaving his team overwhelmed with tasks and not enough clear direction. Ray leaned closer. "You see, Scott, being a leader is more than just working hard or sharing information. It's about setting a direction. It's like flying a plane— you can't just focus on the controls and hope for the best. You need a plan, a destination, and a team that works together. Your team needs that same kind of clarity."

Their talk led them to the airplane hangar, where they both walked inside. There was a surprise waiting—the hangar had an entire office area with a big whiteboard that said, "FLIGHT SCHOOL" in red letters. Ray remained standing while Scott took a seat.

Ray's voice got stronger. "Scott, these days, we're bombarded with emails and texts, all competing for our attention. As a leader, your main job is to cut through the noise about what really matters. And remember, the more important the message, the more often you need to remind them. Just be careful not to overwhelm them with small stuff." Scott understood and nodded.

"There are four primary reasons we need reminders," Ray continued. "Teams need reminders because without them, they will invent their own priorities. When team members create their own priorities, the result is miscommunication, chaos, and confusion. Not everything can have the same importance." Ray began writing the reasons for reminders on the whiteboard, explaining the points as he wrote them:

1. **Reminders help us keep track of our tasks and responsibilities.** "This way, we can stay on top of them and avoid forgetting important deadlines or appointments."

2. **Reminders help us prioritize tasks and make sure we allocate enough time to complete them.** "This can help us be more productive and efficient."

3. **Reminders reduce stress.** "When we have a lot on our plate, it can be easy to feel overwhelmed and anxious. Reminders can help us manage our workload and reduce stress by ensuring we don't forget anything important."

4. **Reminders form habits.** "If we want to form a new habit, such as exercising or meditating, reminders can help us stay on track by prompting us to take action at the right time."

Ray put down his marker and looked at Scott, who was busy writing notes. "Scott, you can't spend all your time on small details." Ray paused. "I agree that it's important to understand your work and your team's efforts in depth, but you also need to remind everyone about the real priorities. Be creative and be relentless!" Scott nodded, showing he understood.

Ray's explanation made sense to him. He knew he had many conflicting priorities in his mind. They talked more about how to incorporate reminders and notifications into the team's daily routine. "There's no one right way to remind effectively, Scott. There are no strict rules. Just try to make reminders a crucial part of your day, every day."

Scott leaned back in his chair and stretched before getting up. Ray's voice signaled the end: "I think we've covered everything for today, Scott."

They both smiled and ended the conversation with a handshake. "Ray, I really appreciate your help!" Scott warmly expressed his thanks.

Ray encouraged him, saying, "I'm always here to support you, Scott!"

As Scott walked back to his car with his notes, he felt excited. He was eager to go back to work with these new insights and renewed enthusiasm.

Scott Reminds His Team

Arriving at the office Monday morning bright and early, Scott was determined to craft his "Reminders" message for the team. He wanted it to be clear and motivating. However, just as he settled in, Gary stormed into the office with a flurry of questions, seemingly ready to pounce. But this time, undeterred by the unexpected interruption, Scott remained confident and composed. Looking Gary in the eye, he calmly but assertively stated, "Gary,

I appreciate your questions, but right now, I need some focused time to work on this message. Could you please give me a bit of space?" His words hung in the air, and despite the initial surprise on Gary's face, Scott's firm stance prevailed, underlining his commitment to the task at hand.

As Gary withdrew, leaving a trail of power dynamics in his wake, Scott worked at his whiteboard where he mapped out a strategy with four distinct reminders for his team:

- A monthly team newsletter, reminding his team of important metrics and achievements.

- A simple 15-minute weekly call with his direct reports covering Key Performance Indicators (KPIs) and their goals for the week.

- A bi-monthly standup team meeting, setting the team's top priorities and discussing obstacles and challenges.

- A day-long offsite leadership retreat where the team would discuss vision and goals in a relaxed environment.

A team motto also emerged in Scott's head: "Propelling Aviation Supplies One Customer at a Time!" He planned to use it as a constant reminder for his team.

Ray's advice kept replaying in his mind, and when the team gathered in the conference room, he sensed some nervousness. But he expected it, knowing there were issues he hadn't reminded them to tackle. Standing up, he took a deep breath and started the meeting differently from before. He shared Ray's words and talked for nearly an hour about changes they would make. He talked quickly at first, feeling anxious, but as he saw nods and smiles, he slowed down. He stopped and asked them for their thoughts.

They spent another hour discussing Scott's ideas. Some team members offered to help in different ways. Judy offered to work on the monthly newsletter. Jim wanted to co-lead the update meetings every two weeks, and Tony knew about and KPI reports. He and Scott planned to meet the next day about them. By the end of the meeting, the nervous feeling was gone and the team actually felt on board. Amy, who always offered her advice, piped in: "Scott, it's nice to finally get some direction!" Her quip was taken both as some criticism and congratulations, but all the same, it was nice to hear some positivity.

Scott breathed a sigh of relief and decided to call his wife.

But before he got the chance, Jackson walked up and said, "Great meeting, Scott, but I have a question."

"Sure, what's that?"

"Why are we doing this? I mean, I love that we're headed in a new direction, but why?"

"What do you mean why, Jackson?" Scott didn't have an answer and told Jackson they would meet soon about that.

Scott Asks Ray, "Why?"

Scott left the office earlier than usual and headed over to locate Ray. "Hey, Ray. How's everything going today?" He proceeded to fill Ray in on the creation of his reminders and the details of the team meeting.

Ray seemed pleased, giving Scott a friendly pat on the shoulder. "Great job, buddy."

"I do have a question, though. Someone on my team asked me about the purpose behind all of this. It struck me as a solid question, and I figured maybe you could help me come up with an answer."

"Ah, yes! Let's discuss that next Saturday morning," Ray suggested. They spent some time chatting about the progress of the restoration work on the old airplane, and then Scott headed back to his office.

As the following week unfolded and Scott witnessed swift and encouraging results, his eagerness grew for Saturday's conversation with Ray, an anticipation underscored by the improvements he was observing. Stepping back into the hangar, the whiteboard was once again full of more information, dominated by the conspicuous header "WHY?" Beneath it was a geometric diagram in the shape of a mountain peak, bearing the word "PEAK" as its caption.

"Hey, Scott, today we're talking about the 'why' of things," Ray started. "Sometimes leaders forget how important it is to keep reminding their teams not just about where they're headed, but also why they're on that journey. In our last talk, we saw how reminders can be really helpful, which is great. But to make a real change, we need to go beyond the 'what' and dig into the 'why,'" he finished, pointing to the mysterious picture on the whiteboard.

Teams Need PEAK Reminders

"Teams need to be reminded of their four PEAK principles: Purpose, Expectations, Accountability, and Keep It Simple. When you put these four principles into action, you'll watch your team grow in effectiveness. Today, we'll discuss the first principle: Purpose." Ray wrote "Purpose" on the whiteboard.

"A team can't be a team until the members know *why* they are a team. A team is made up of many different and unique individuals. Each person has a unique personality and characteristics, and unless a leader finds a way to get them working together, they end up working against each other. Knowing your team's purpose is important because it gives direction and meaning to your work. Purpose is the heart of the team's story, and here are some of its attributes." Ray wrote five items on the whiteboard, explaining as he wrote them:

1. **Clarity.** "When a team knows its purpose, the members have a clearer understanding of what they want to achieve in life. This clarity can help them make better decisions and stay focused on what's important."

2. **Motivation.** "Having a clear purpose provides a sense of motivation and drive. When a team has a meaningful goal, it can inspire every member to work hard and persevere through challenges."

3. **Prioritization.** "When a team knows its purpose, it prioritizes time and energy on

the things that matter most to the team. This helps to avoid distractions and to focus on what's truly most important."

4. **Fulfillment.** "When a team is working purposefully, every member feels more fulfilled and satisfied. Having a sense of purpose can give a sense of accomplishment and make all members feel that they are making a difference at work."

5. **A sense of identity.** "A purpose can provide a group with a sense of identity and belonging. When everyone is working toward a common goal, it can create a sense of community and shared values."

Scott Becomes a Storyteller

After discussing the significance of purpose, Ray transitioned into the concept of creating purpose through storytelling. "Scott, the most effective way to help your team members grasp their purpose and to ignite their enthusiasm for their work is through storytelling. That's where they'll find purpose. Storytelling is one of the most essential tools in a leader's toolbox, and if executed skillfully and appropriately, the impact of a compelling story will be substantial. It will motivate, invigorate, and forge a potent sense of connection. It will propel your team from passivity to action. Scott, don't underestimate how vital this is." Scott listened attentively, jotting down notes as Ray spoke.

"I've got a task for you, Scott. I want you to pen down your story. Share your team's purpose in a way that's genuine and captivating. Craft it into something that people will be eager to share with others."

"But I'm not much of a storyteller, Ray," Scott objected.

"That's not true at all. We're all storytellers, Scott. Consider how many times each day you recount your experiences to others. Remember the last time you described a fantastic movie, a captivating book, or an exhilarating basketball game to a friend. Everyone possesses the ability to tell stories."

Scott paused and nodded, finding the logic in Ray's words. They continued their conversation, during which Ray recounted a personal story about the airplane he was restoring.

"My uncle Ted taught me how to fly in this old plane. Ted had a passion for the skies, spending as much time as he could soaring into the wide blue expanse. I watched him take off and land until he eventually sat me in the back cockpit. That's when I fell in love with flying, too. They say that once aviation captures your heart, it's a lifelong attachment. Despite its ups and downs like any relationship, it's a thrilling journey that I'll never give up." Ray's voice wavered slightly, and a tear formed in his eye. "The last time I saw Ted, the old plane crashed a few hundred yards that way," Ray pointed to the southwest. "It was our last flight together." A moment of silence followed, during which Scott remained quiet. "That's my story, Scott. That's why I invest so much care and effort into *Boomerang*, and it's why I'm determined to restore it and take off once more. It's all for Ted." Scott nodded, and after a brief pause, he walked away while Ray resumed his work. It was a lesson that Scott would always carry with him.

Monday morning, as Scott sat at his desk, he contemplated his team's purpose and story. Prior to his conversation with Ray the previous day, he hadn't given much thought to the subjects. However, Ray's story deeply moved him. Now he comprehended why Ray labored diligently and with such dedication on that aging plane. So Scott embarked on crafting his own narrative—the tale of the members of his team and their *raison d'être*, their purpose. It occupied the remainder of the day, and he eagerly anticipated presenting it to his team on Friday.

Scott's Purpose Message

A few days later, Scott assembled his team in the conference room. A blend of nerves and excitement coursed through him as he took the lead, ready to share his story.

"Team," he started, "every one of us takes to the skies by airplane, perhaps several times a year. I recall a flight to visit my grandfather before he passed away last year—a man who meant the world to me, and whose absence I feel deeply. Or the time I flew with my family to witness the majesty of the Grand Canyon, an experience etched forever in my heart. You've surely noticed the photographs on my office walls. I'm certain that each of you can reflect on a cherished moment that would have remained a distant dream had you not embarked on a flight that safely delivered you to your destination. Life is defined by our journeys—our arrivals by airplane."

Scott glanced into the eyes of his team members as he spoke. He felt his message was resonating, or at least he was gaining some acceptance. He continued.

"Today, I ask each of you to take a moment to contemplate one special memory that owes its existence to a flight you've taken. As we're all aware, the airline industry of today is in constant flux. Sourcing new parts has become a difficult challenge for us, and without our efforts, some planes would simply remain grounded. We locate high-quality used and generic components to keep the jets soaring, allowing these memories to continue. It's no small task, a reality we face daily. It requires a cohesive team—our team—to track down these crucial parts and to ensure they find their way to the right hangar. And with every accomplishment, we contribute to craft cherished memories for individuals out there."

Scott's team members nodded their heads in agreement. Someone encouraged him to continue. "That's true, Scott." This made him feel more confident.

He concluded, "Amidst the hustle and, yes, the stress that comes with it, let's not lose sight of our initial purpose. We are the creators of memories. Let that remain steadfast in your minds! I urge each of you to locate a photograph from a journey you've taken on an airplane. These images will be framed and showcased on the walls of our conference room, serving as a constant reminder."

Scott had guarded optimism when he headed into his presentation, but now he was elated with the response from his team. His speech sparked all sorts of conversation from his team members, both personal and professional. But the best part was the personal interaction. Over the next few days, the team had fun sharing stories and photographs. The memories shared between them bonded the team in a brand new way, and it connected their lives with their work in a way that improved cooperation and motivation. It was the spark that Scott was looking for, and he could hardly wait to tell Ray.

"If team members don't
know what to expect, they'll
make up tasks on their own,
causing chaos."

7

What to Expect Beyond Purpose

On Saturday morning, Scott met up with Ray at the hangar, and he was really excited. "Ray, I can't thank you enough. The team is getting along so much better, and it's happening in ways I didn't expect," Scott said with a proud smile.

Ray smiled back and took a seat. "Sit down, Scott, and tell me all about it." They talked and Scott shared his speech and described how the team bonded, all because they had a strong sense of purpose. Ray congratulated him, and they started talking about the team's progress in different areas.

"You've achieved remarkable strides, Scott. I'm genuinely proud of you," Ray commended sincerely. Yet, he noted, there was more to be accomplished. "We're not done yet." A deliberate stride carried Ray back toward the whiteboard, upon which he scripted a bold message: EXPECTATIONS.

"Ray, where are we headed now?" Scott asked.

Ray responded, "While a team's purpose marks a significant leap toward tangible progress, unless they're aware of your expectations, that very progress might slip through your fingers." The concept seemed to leave Scott slightly adrift. Ray continued, "Let me sketch it out for you, Scott." He began writing on the whiteboard while he explained:

- **Understanding.** "Ensure everyone understands what's expected of them and the way they should behave in the workplace. You should embed this in your supervision of the team and in ongoing learning and development."

- **Alignment.** "To ensure these norms align with your work culture, everyone on the team should understand your company's mission and values. These need to be directly and succinctly communicated, and done regularly."

- **Direction.** "If team members don't know what to expect work, they'll make up tasks on their own, which will eventually cause chaos and loss of direction. A team on purpose is effective, but a team with purpose and expectation is powerful."

- **Shared values.** "The foundation for expectations is shared values. Every member of a team needs to understand the fundamental beliefs, concepts, and principles that underlie the culture of an organization. These values guide all decisions and behaviors. This is what links organizations together."

Scott commented, "I grasp the concept, Ray, at least in theory. It sounds promising. But how and where exactly should I begin?" His curiosity was tinged with a hint of uncertainty.

"It's not as daunting as it might seem, Scott." Ray responded, detailing several approaches through which Scott could set expectations that would propel his team forward. "Now, bear in mind that I'm not advocating for micromanagement. That's what your boss, Gary, does. You don't want to cultivate an atmosphere where you're perpetually hovering. That doesn't sit well with anyone. Rather, I'm suggesting you create your own set of 'commitments.' That way, there's no need to breathe down everyone's neck." Ray shared further insights, guiding Scott on where to commence.

With their conversation drawing to a close, Ray sent Scott off with a mission. Scott delved into the task of crafting a shared set of values for his team, a blueprint to ensure that they all would comprehend what to anticipate when they stepped through the doors each morning.

Shared Values and Expectations

When Scott arrived at work the next day, he found the team in the conference room looking at each other's photographs on the memory wall while chatting and laughing. The sense of bonding and engagement between staff members was a 360-degree turnaround from even a few weeks before. Scott sat down at the conference table and spoke a silent "YES!" to himself, and then Gary strolled in.

Scott was nervous because the team wasn't directly engaged in work, and indeed Gary asked why everyone wasn't working. "Why is everyone standing around and chatting, Scott?" Gary demanded in front of the team. Then he barked several more orders.

Scott listened and acknowledged Gary, and then he told his boss that he was "on it." But he also did something surprising. In an unexpected turn, Scott decided to involve Gary in a different way during the team meeting.

Scott approached Gary and suggested, "Hey, Gary, how about you share your favorite air flight memory with the team? It could be a nice way for everyone to get to know you better."

Surprisingly, Gary agreed, albeit with a hint of hesitation and awkwardness. As he started talking, his initial uncertainty transformed into something different. He recounted a personal memory about flying to witness his son's graduation from the Air Force Academy. As he spoke, he was taken aback by some of the emotion in his own words, revealing a side of himself that the team had rarely seen. But when his account ended, Gary quickly reverted back to his former self and told everyone to get back to work. Scott, pleased with his little ploy, headed back to his cubicle to work on his "Expectations" message with his team.

But Scott was having a hard time writing the message. He admitted to himself that he could use some help. He remembered Ray telling him to lean on others. He emphasized that it was important not to pretend to have all the answers or to know everything, as Gary did. Instead, he encouraged Scott to be open to seeking assistance and collaborating with his team and colleagues. So Scott decided to get the other senior managers involved in a discussion. He called a meeting and explained why the company needed to do a better job of communicating with the staff about expectations.

When they all sit down, Scott talked about his ideas and asked for their thoughts. The atmosphere became engaging and the managers started sharing their own ideas. They built on each other's thoughts, and teamwork not only brought out new creative ideas, but it also helped them feel closer as a management team. By the end of the meeting, Scott was happy because he gained valuable feedback that would make his message to the team even better. He also started to understand how working together like this could make a big difference. The best part was that the management team felt a certain buy-in. He even received a high-five from the IT director!

Scott's Expectations Message

As Scott prepared for his team meeting, he felt confident and hopeful. He and the other senior managers worked hard to put together a message that would take Scott's team to the next level. He had begun to notice some positive changes happening already, and the previous discussions made him even more confident that his message would make sense to everyone. He was also excited that some of the senior managers volunteered to attend the meeting as well, adding to Scott's confidence.

He stood at the front of the conference table and proceeded. "Team, we talked about our story, the reasons we do what we do when we come to work every day. It's been sheer joy to see us come together and celebrate our purpose. Today, I want to talk to you about the shared expectations we have for each other—our shared values. We've never talked about this, and I think you'll be encouraged to know that we're taking the next step beyond purpose. I've created what I think ought to be our expectations here at work:

"Number one, respect each other, be willing to help each other instead of displaying an 'it's not my job' attitude.

"Second, be efficient, because our outcomes depend on speed.

"Third, be flexible about your work and tasks.

"Number four, don't be afraid to ask or offer help when needed."

Scott continued with great enthusiasm. "Imagine when you arrive at work every morning if you know beyond a shadow of a doubt that each of us would commit to living out these expectations. Imagine the unity we'd develop together as a team. Rather than fight with each other, resist each other, and object to each other's ideas and work, we'd come to work with common expectations. This is what will link us together in a practical way and take us from a team on purpose to a team that has each other's back. When the day gets tough and we're under stress and pressure, let's stand back to back and agree to watch out for each other!"

Scott paused, inhaling deeply as he surveyed the room, and he caught glances exchanged among his team members. Amidst the suspense, a tentative silence lingered until a voice broke through the uncertainty. "Scott," declared Pete, "I believe we get it. Shared purpose, shared values. Count me in!"

The room seemed to sway in agreement as heads nodded in unison, culminating in a lively high-five exchanged between two other team members.

Scott experienced something he was not accustomed to. It wasn't just from working really hard. He now realized that being a real leader wasn't just about working nonstop. It was also about helping them all understand that they were working together for the same reasons. As they started talking about airplane parts in the meeting, there was a strong feeling of togetherness. The team members were all finally on the same page. Thinking about what Ray might say made Scott really proud.

"When employees are accountable for their work, they are more likely to take ownership."

8

Ray Keeps Scott Accountable

Ray sat outside the hangar, basking in the warmth of the sun, when Scott approached with excitement. The day was awash in sunshine, and Ray's progress on the airplane was becoming increasingly tangible, hinting at the possibility of it once more gracing the skies. "Impressive work you've done there, Ray," Scott exclaimed. "I'm starting to think your vision of getting this old plane airborne isn't so far-fetched after all."

Ray's grin matched Scott's enthusiasm, punctuated by a hearty slap on the back. "So, spill the beans, Scott. What's the latest from the office?"

In response, Scott detailed how he had introduced the team to their shared values, recounting the impact it had on their newfound ability to collaboratively troubleshoot. He added that even his boss, Gary, had taken note of the team's heightened productivity, evidenced by their increased parts sourcing and delivery in comparison to previous weeks.

"You've done it, Scott!" Ray's exclamation echoed their collective achievement.

Scott, seizing a chair, settled into it with a triumphant smile, inhaling deeply. "Seems like my task is completed, Ray. Now that we've got our purpose and expectations aligned, I can see everything naturally falling into place."

Ray's response was candid. "I wish it were that simple."

As Ray began to move toward the hangar, Scott's expression was quizzical. "We're not finished yet, Scott. Come along," Ray beckoned. Inside the hangar, the bold letters "ACCOUNTABILITY" dominated the whiteboard.

Scott took a seat, focusing on Ray and his whiteboard. Ray started explaining the subject in his usual clear way. He explained that even if all team members know what they're supposed to do and what's expected, they can still go off track if they're not responsible for their actions. He talked more about this, saying how accountability is vital to keep the team on the right path and to keep everyone honest. They also talked about how making sure everyone takes responsibility will stop team members from blaming each other. Ray began again by writing on the whiteboard and explaining each point about accountability:

- **Is critical for effective decision-making.** "When employees are held accountable for their decisions, they are more likely to make informed and well-thought-out choices. This is because they understand that their decisions will be scrutinized and evaluated based on the outcomes they produce. In this way, accountability helps to ensure that employees take their decision-making responsibilities seriously and that they consider the impact of their decisions on the organization as a whole."

- **Promotes a sense of responsibility and commitment.** "When employees are accountable for their work, they are more likely to take ownership of their tasks and to be committed to achieving organizational goals. This is because they understand that their performance will be evaluated based on their ability to deliver on their commitments."

- **Is crucial for ensuring that the organization operates in an ethical and responsible manner.** "When employees are accountable for their actions, they are less likely to engage in unethical behavior or to take short-cuts. It keeps everyone honest because they understand that their actions will be evaluated based on the organization's values and principles."

"Genius!" Scott exclaimed as he listened and took notes. He wrote furiously until he'd written everything down, and then he stood up and quickly darted out the hangar door.

"Wait, Scott, I'm not finished!" Ray shouted.

But it was too late as Scott was so excited to begin the next step, he started jogging back to the office. But he turned around as he moved toward the building and away from the hanger. "See you soon, Ray. Don't worry—I understand!" Scott then walked back into the office, sat at his desk, and hammered out an email to his team:

Subject Line: New Accountability Program

Team, I'm creating a new accountability program to help us stay on task. Please use my calendar link below to schedule a day and time to meet with me. During our meeting, I'll talk to each of you about what you're accountable for and to whom, and then we'll discuss penalties or disciplinary actions if you fail to meet the criteria I've established. I'm excited to see each of you become more accountable!

One by one, Scott's team members walked into his office and listened to his accountability message. He talked to each of them about how important it was to keep each other on task and that it was his job to make sure of it: "Accountability is going to be enforced around here," he told them. At the end of the day, he took a deep breath and smiled to himself. Once again, he took Ray's lessons to the table and turned his team around. It wouldn't be long before Gary noticed once again his leadership abilities. It was Friday afternoon, and Scott strolled out early to go tell his wife.

"You want the team to feel
like they're winning,
not losing. Everyone needs
to feel rewarded."

9

A Disastrous Week for the Drill Sergeant

Monday morning, Scott rushed out of his house, prepared to make sure everyone was being held accountable, just as Ray explained it to him. It was another magic bullet, Scott told himself.

However, his excitement turned into dismay as soon as he reached the office. Two of his teammates wanted to talk to him, and they were both angry. Then another teammate was upset with someone else on the team. He spent the whole day dealing with their problems and trying to make people feel better. This happened every day during that week, and Scott's plans to make everyone responsible for their work didn't seem to be working. His accountability efforts seemed to have created a "blame game" with his team. He was not happy about this because up until now, he had always found Ray's advice to work wonders.

Sitting at his desk, he wondered what went wrong. Just then, his best employee, Greg, entered his office and sat down. He looked him in the eye and asked, "Scott, why would anyone feel like working for a company that doesn't trust its employees?"

Scott didn't say anything as Greg added, "Everything was going really well for us, but now it feels like someone is constantly watching over us. What's the reason behind this?"

Scott apologized to Greg and suggested that he leave early that day. He told him, "Let's all get together on Monday morning and talk about it." Scott knew it had been a train wreck and that he had to pull back.

This time when he arrived home, he walked past his wife and up to his room. He was so exhausted, he went to sleep and didn't wake up until Saturday morning.

Scott then drove to the airport to see Ray, who noticed immediately that Scott's attitude had turned sour as he stood with arms crossed and a resentful look on his face. "Scott, I told you I wasn't finished. Don't tell me you became the office drill sergeant! Sit down, and let's talk."

Scott sat and admitted that the week was a disaster. "Accountability isn't working like you suggested it would, Ray."

"Scott, this isn't about discipline or giving orders. It's about establishing specific and measurable outcomes for everyone on the team, making sure that everyone understands those outcomes, and then finding ways to collaboratively discuss those outcomes. You left before I had a chance to explain this to you!"

Ray shared more. "This is what can happen when you act like a 'big brother.' This term describes your behavior when you are overbearing, controlling, and intrusive toward others. It can cause you to take on a paternalistic role, in which you believe you know what is best for others and you try to dictate their actions and decisions. This behavior can have negative consequences for both you and those on the receiving end of your actions.

"Scott, acting like a big brother disempowers and undermines the autonomy of others. When you act this way, it causes resentment and frustration, as your team members feel that their decisions and choices are not valued or respected. Do you think this is possibly how your team members felt last week?"

Scott nodded yes.

"When you are constantly overbearing and controlling, it creates a dynamic that is unhealthy and unproductive. It causes tension and conflict in relationships, as those on the receiving end feel that they aren't being heard or respected. This leads to a breakdown in communication and a lack of trust, which can be difficult to repair."

"Do you think it's too late, Ray? Did I ruin everything?" Scott asked.

"Not at all," Ray replied, "but you should move quickly. Go back to the office and apologize. Take responsibility for it, and you'll be surprised at how forgiving your team will be. They're just as excited about the progress as you are, and they want to get things back on track as well."

Scott breathed a sigh of relief and then asked, "So what then? If you say accountability is so important, what steps do I take?"

Ray walked back to the whiteboard and wrote down three words:

POWER

CONTROL

SUPPORT

Ray explained, "For some, the word 'account-ability' stands for the idea of POWER. This looks like a control freak boss that micromanages their team. Such a boss keeps people accountable through fear or intimidation instead of through rapport building or relationship. For others, the idea of account-ability equals CONTROL. It looks like checking in on every single step, looking over everyone's shoulders. In this sort of situation, there's no room for creativity or innovation. It stifles the team. POWER and CONTROL won't move your team forward.

"Does this sound like someone you know, Scott?"

Scott immediately recognizes Gary but doesn't say anything.

"Does it have the opposite effect on you, Scott?"

He nodded and replied, "Yes. It actually has the opposite effect." He then asked, "So what, Ray? How does it work instead?"

Ray returned to the whiteboard:

LISTEN + CARE + SUPPORT = ACCOUNTABILITY THAT WINS

"Scott, we're looking for balance here. You want the team to feel that they're winning, not losing. Everyone on your team needs to feel rewarded when work gets done well. They all need to know you're

no

there for them, and that they are there for you. Accountability goes both ways because managers are just as accountable to the employees as the other way around. Listen, care, and support your team, and everyone will feel invested in the future. That's the kind of accountability that will increase your productivity and creativity."

Suddenly, the idea that accountability wasn't about discipline but about reward made sense to Scott. Ray shared a bit more while they walked back to the airplane. "It looks like you've been working on the engine, Ray."

"Indeed I have, and by next week she'll be roaring to life once again. I can hardly wait!" They smiled at each other, and Scott turned to walk back to the office.

The idea of supporting the team really appealed to Scott, and it was certainly going to be more fun than to deliver bad news or to administer discipline.

"Simplicity fosters a collaborative environment where employees can contribute without unnecessary obstacles."

10

Scott Wins Again

That evening, Scott told his wife what had happened over the past week, including the mini-disaster he created, but also how Ray was helping him recover. "You've never been a quitter, Scott, and I know you'll turn things around." Indeed, that was his plan. Scott and Sarah looked at each other and smiled. The last weeks and months had been challenging, to say the least. The next afternoon he would meet with Gary again, which he was nervous about, but he was also eager for it because he knew Gary couldn't help but notice his team's success. Numbers don't lie!

Scott spent the next morning mending fences with his team. He immediately gathered the employees together and apologized for his military-style accountability program. He saluted them and jokingly told them to salute back, and of course everyone laughed. When the tension was broken, he announced a new plan, which he didn't even call an "accountability plan" but instead a "back to back" plan, meaning they all would have each other's back. He reminded the team members that their purpose was to help people fly to their destination safely and on time, and that to do that, "We all must have each other's back." Scott's new plan involved restructured regular team meetings to discuss what was going right so everyone could participate in the team's victories, but also to discuss what was going wrong. When failures would arise, Scott would open the floor to discussions about how the team could look at the data, be more proactive, and make smarter decisions. "The environment will be super positive and encouraging, giving everyone the opportunity to celebrate together and also to problem-solve together. We're accountable to each other here, which shows we care," Scott told the team in closing.

The message was well received, and the team members left the conference room encouraged and ready to nurture each other toward more productivity!

Gary Makes Things Complicated

Scott walked into Gary's office, where his boss was buried in reports. He didn't say anything when Scott sat down. They were both silent for a few minutes as Gary continued to browse a pile of spreadsheets. Scott was nervous because Gary looked confused.

"Scott, I'm not sure these reports are accurate," Gary said when he looked up.

"Why so?" Scott replied. He knew the reports were accurate, but he played dumb.

"I just don't understand how things could have turned around so quickly. These numbers are outstanding," said Gary.

Scott took time before the meeting to review all of the spreadsheets, so he knew them backward and forward. He immediately jumped in and explained to Gary in detail why and how the numbers looked so good. Gary simply sat and listened while Scott described in great detail how his team had executed so well. He also described what Ray had taught him, but he never mentioned his mentor's name.

"My team has a purpose, Gary, a reason for doing what we do each day. All of my team members understand why they're in the game. And as you're aware, we have a story to tell, a purpose for doing what we do. I've also built in expectations so that every member of my team understands what the company expects, particularly in terms of our values," Scott explained. Gary didn't reply, but he let Scott keep talking. "Gary, we look out for each other. We trust each other and hold each other accountable." Gary was still silent and stared at Scott as if he had no idea what he was talking about. Scott just smiled. The numbers spoke for themselves.

Gary paused for a little while longer and then looked down, grabbed a file, and handed it to Scott. "Scott, these are some new policies and procedures, and I need you and your team to start referring to them every day. It's imperative that we as a company begin to raise the bar in terms of how we're going about our work. Learn this material, and make sure your team does the same. Let me be clear: this isn't a suggestion. It's a requirement." Gary said all of this in his typical know-it-all boss fashion.

Scott didn't argue with him but took the folders as he agreed to study Gary's new policies and procedures. Gary looked down and returned to work without saying anything else. Scott stood up and began to walk out the door, but then he paused briefly and looked back at his boss. "Have a super day!" Gary didn't look up.

When Scott returned to his desk, he browsed through the files Gary handed him. Inside he found copious notes with many detailed instructions. It must have taken Gary many weeks to compile such a list. He certainly was a glutton for detail, but since Gary was his boss, Scott pushed ahead and met with his team. They literally spent the better part of the day reviewing each and every item Gary asked for, which essentially was compiled into a long list of "documentation." It appeared that he wanted team members to document every action that would be taken each day, and practically every word that would be said. Well, it wasn't quite that bad, but he did insist that the team spend a great deal of time making a record of their work.

Scott wasn't naïve, and he knew that Gary's thirst for documentation would stifle the team's morale as well as their creativity. It might also lead to some team infighting ("Hey, you forgot to document that!"). Too much documentation would simply paper over organizational or personnel issues. Indeed, during Scott's meeting with his team, someone raised his voice and astutely observed that Gary had invented a "process fix" for a people problem. "Scott, I don't think we have a problem with our process. If we have a problem, it's just getting the team better motivated and organized around the work each day," said Bill. They all worked together the rest of the day and then left the office and went home. But Scott didn't go home. He took a walk to the hangar and sat down with Ray.

"Ray, Gary has really thrown another wrench into my work. He's demanding too much reporting and too much detail. I'm gonna lose my head!"

Ray doesn't miss a beat. He walked over to his whiteboard and wrote three words:

Keep It Simple

Ray talked to Scott about the importance of reducing everything at work to bite-sized nuggets that were easy to consume. "Rather than going full throttle with detail, do the opposite. Reduce the fractions, Scott—don't expand them," he said. "Now, this doesn't mean you shouldn't have a manual or guidebook. A full airplane manual has hundreds of pages, but the pilot isn't paging through them before each flight. Instead, we do a complete but simple 'pre-flight,' which is simply a visual walk-around of the airplane. Then we jump into the cockpit and locate the flight control column, more commonly called the yoke. The systems and gauges look pretty complicated, but in reality, they're not. It doesn't take much to control a plane. We simply locate the throttle, browse about seven flight instruments, find the landing gear control, and place our feet on the rudder panels, and pretty soon, we're airborne!

"I'm not saying it's simple, and neither is your work, Scott. But neither a pilot nor a manager should have to spend much time in the manual. You should spend most of your time with what's most important and not the details that are irrelevant to the task at hand." Ray stood up and wrote three questions on the whiteboard:

- Will it be better for our customers?

- Will it make it safer for our people?

- Will it improve our company's position?

"Try to narrow it all down to these three questions, Scott. If what you're doing goes above and beyond these three questions, you might consider spending less time on it. Simplifying your work processes and tasks reduces complexity, streamlines operations, and eliminates unnecessary steps. This leads to increased efficiency and productivity, and it will lessen stress around the office. When tasks are straightforward and easy to understand, employees can complete them more quickly and with fewer errors, saving time and resources. Simplicity fosters a collaborative environment where employees can contribute their ideas and expertise without unnecessary obstacles."

Scott intuitively knew this, but Ray's words always motivated him to take action. He walked back to the office not only ready to tell his team, but also to tell Gary. He was keeping it simple from now on!

"A collaborative environment
is possible only when
everyone's opinions
hold weight."

11

Scott's Team Turns It Around

Scott didn't allow himself to be intimidated by Gary's presence any longer. Now when they met, Scott's newfound self-assuredness shone through, and he addressed Gary's questions with confidence. Despite Scott's openness in sharing his experiences and the guidance he received from his mentor, Ray, Gary remained puzzled by the remarkable turnaround the company had witnessed under Scott's leadership. The inexplicable shift in Scott's approach and the success he achieved continued to baffle Gary, leaving him grappling with how Scott had managed to effect such positive change.

Since Dave's passing, the atmosphere in the office had been charged with tension as two distinct leadership approaches clashed head-on. Gary and Scott, both hard-working and determined, couldn't have been more different in their styles.

Gary, the seasoned traditionalist, held onto the reins of control with an iron grip. He firmly believed in maintaining a top-down hierarchy, where his authority was never to be questioned. The employees, while compliant, often felt stifled under his watchful eye. On the opposite side of the spectrum stood Scott, the advocate for a different kind of culture, one in which people came first.

Ray helped Scott foster a collaborative environment where everyone's opinions held weight. Scott learned to encourage open discussions and creative thinking. Instead of imposing his ideas, he facilitated brainstorming sessions that gave birth to innovative solutions. His office was always open for discussions, and his team thrived in an atmosphere of trust and empowerment. People were reminded of what to do, when to do it, and how to do it. Most importantly, they understood their purpose and willingly held each other accountable.

Gary delivered results, no doubt, but at a cost—creativity and problem-solving were stifled.

In contrast, Scott's team, while initially slower to produce, showcased a remarkable increase in engagement and job satisfaction. The office buzzed with energy as team members freely shared their ideas and collaborated on projects. The stark difference between the two approaches couldn't be ignored. Yet Ray wasn't finished with Scott. He was transformed, but there was still a lot of room left on the runway for improvement!

Meanwhile, Scott saw that Ray was diligently dedicating his time and expertise to the meticulous restoration of his beloved airplane, and his efforts were bearing tangible fruit. The wings, once weathered and worn, were now reattached and gleaming with fresh coats of paint. The fuselage had been painstakingly restored to its former glory. The propeller, once rusted and stationary, had been meticulously overhauled. Each blade had been carefully inspected, repaired, and balanced, a laborious process that showcased Ray's keen attention to detail. His passion for aviation and his dedication to the project were evident in every facet of the restoration, and with each passing day, he brought his vision of airborne revival closer to reality.

"I've got some exciting news. I think our airplane is almost ready for flight!" Ray proclaimed the next time Scott dropped by.

"Really? That's incredible, Ray! You mean all the hard work and countless hours we've put into it are finally paying off?"

"Absolutely! The wings are restored to their former glory, the propeller is spinning smoothly, and the engine is purring like a cat. It won't be long now before she takes to the skies again."

"That's amazing to hear, Ray. I can't believe how far we've come. So when do we get to see her in action?"

"Well, here's the plan. I want you to come see me again next Saturday morning. I've set up a schedule for some final checks and tests, and if everything goes well, we might just have a test flight on the horizon."

Scott was elated. He nodded and headed back to the office, looking forward to his next visit.

SECTION 3

Routines

"When routines are embedded into a team's culture, they align with your team's shared values and goals."

12

Ray and Scott Go Flying

Scott arrived at the airport at sunrise. He'd flown in many commercial planes throughout his life, but never a small plane. He patiently waited for Ray while standing beside the restored plane that would soon carry them both through the skies like a soaring bird. He was proud to have helped tear the old plane apart and put it back together, while also exploring with Ray new dimensions of team building. This morning, unbeknownst to him, he'd soon learn more about lifting off than meeting the sky. Once again, Scott's time with Ray would take on new directions.

As Scott waited, he pondered the wealth of knowledge that Ray had eagerly shared with him over the past few months. He was beginning to wonder about this old man. For someone who fixed and restored antique planes, he possessed more leadership savvy than anyone he'd ever met. Who was he? Nevertheless, when Ray arrived, he wasted no time and launched right into his pre-flight check, emphasizing to Scott the importance of the routine.

"Scott," Ray began, his voice filled with his usual sense of purpose, "before we embark on this journey together, let's make sure that she's ready for the skies. You can't ever assume too much. We've got to stick to the routine."

"What routine is that, Ray?"

Ray led Scott through the intricate dance of the pre-flight check routine. They started by inspecting the exterior of the aircraft, their hands gliding over the sleek surface. Ray demonstrated how to scan for any blemishes or signs of damage that could jeopardize the flight. Scott followed suit, his fingertips tracing the contours of the plane with care and attention.

Next, Ray directed Scott's focus to the two wings, the very appendages that would lift them to new heights. They scrutinized the rivets and fasteners, ensuring that each one was secure. Ray taught Scott how to assess the integrity of the control surfaces, ensuring their freedom of movement and responsiveness. Every little detail mattered, and Scott absorbed Ray's words.

As they moved closer to the heart of the aircraft, Ray explained the intricacies of the engine compartment. They examined the cowling, verifying the tightness of each fastener. Scott learned to check the

propeller for any signs of wear or imbalance, understanding the impact such nuances could have on
the flight experience. Then, inside the cockpit, Ray
shared about the instrument panel and its gauges.
There were twelve gauges, and together they tested
each one, ensuring accurate readings. Scott was a bit
overwhelmed, but Ray was patient with him. "We
can't skip any steps here, Scott; we've got to stick to
the routine."

In the cockpit as Ray again emphasized the
significance of the pre-flight check routine, he
paused, looked at Scott, and said with all seriousness,
"Routines are the foundation upon which success is
built, both in the air and everywhere else, for that
matter." He explained that routines provide the
structure and consistency that propel individuals and
teams toward success. "Intentional routines create
stability and consistency that nurtures a culture of
excellence. Without them, people usually wander
off-track and end up further away from their goals."

Scott took mental notes while Ray moved on.
His patient instruction extended to the vital systems
that sustained flight. They checked the fuel quantity
and confirmed the proper functioning of the elec-
trical system. Scott learned to ensure that emergency
equipment was readily accessible, appreciating the
peace of mind it provided. The depth and detail of

the pre-flight routine surprised Scott. From examining the communication systems to scrutinizing the navigation instruments, every step in the pre-flight check unfolded like a symphony of precision.

"There's a lot to remember here, Ray. What if we miss a step?" asked Scott.

"Good question, so before we jump in and lift off, let's take a gander over to the hangar. I want to show you something."

Scott nodded, and they walked together into the hangar where the aroma of aviation fuel mingled with the spirit of possibility. Scott sat down in front of the whiteboard where Ray had already scrawled on the whiteboard:

ROUTINES: A collection of habits that shape outcomes. Routines are norms of behavior, whether intentional or unintentional, that ultimately create our future.

Plan

Act

Reflect

Wasting no time, Ray began teaching Scott once again, his voice carrying the weight of experience. "Routines are the backbone of success, both in the skies and on the ground. They must not be meaningless, repetitive actions. They are intentional habits that enable us to navigate complexity and achieve our goals, and they provide the structure necessary to weather storms and seize opportunities, both in the air and in the workplace."

Scott's brow furrowed with curiosity. "Ray, I believe you," he interjected, "but my team has a great sense of purpose and a big vision. Isn't that enough?"

"Not usually, Scott. In the workplace, routines act like the pistons in our airplane engines. When they all fire together at the right time, it's time to lift off! They foster the accountability needed not only to begin the job, but also to finish it. When routines become embedded within a team's culture, they align with your team's shared values and goals."

Scott nodded, beginning to grasp what Ray was trying to teach him.

"Success is more than just dreams and visions, Scott. Without good habits and routines, you'll never lift off. As a leader, the routines you establish provide the framework for consistency, which leads to trust. They create a rhythm that instills a sense of security and clarity within the team. Other times, there might be some bad habits that are holding your team back. It goes both ways."

"Can you give me an example?" asked Scott.

"Let me ask you this question. When you're in a meeting with Gary, who does most of the talking, you or Gary?"

"Well, Gary, of course," replied Scott.

"And how does that make you feel?"

"It makes me feel like I don't matter, like my ideas don't matter."

"Exactly!" proclaimed Ray. "So when you meet with your team or with individual team members, make it your routine to do the opposite. Make it a habit to ask for feedback and to listen to their ideas."

Scott nodded in agreement. He liked that idea. His mind was racing, connecting the dots between routines and effective leadership.

"Scott, routines are more than a collection of tasks. They are the building blocks of a thriving culture—the stronger and more aligned the routines, the stronger and more aligned the culture. When powerful routines are integrated into the DNA of a team, they become your secret sauce that weaves everything together. Embrace routines, nurture them, and watch as they transform not only your own leadership effectiveness, but also the lives of those you guide."

Scott took a moment to let Ray's words sink in. The significance of routines resonated within him, transforming his perspective on leadership and the workplace. Routines are the stuff dreams are made of. They create an environment that nurtures talent, inspires creativity, and fosters a shared commitment to success, or they tear it down. Scott had worked hard with his team on creating a sense of purpose, but he admitted that they didn't build routines along the way to keep everyone on track. Maybe this was the piece that seemed to be missing, aligning actual actions that would bring purpose to their work.

Ray grabbed his goggles and began to walk out of the hangar. "There's more, Scott, but now it's time to lift off!" He smiled and walked toward the plane.

As Scott stood beside the aircraft, his heart pounded with anticipation. Today, he would take to the skies with Ray in an old junk piece of aircraft that looked like it would never see a runway once again. But they restored it together, and Ray had become a mentor to Scott, sharing his wealth of knowledge and experience. Now, he would guide Scott through the pivotal moments leading up to takeoff. He could hardly wait. They both donned their goggles, but Ray paused again before starting the engine, and he started talking about routines again.

"Scott," Ray began, "about those other three words I wrote on the whiteboard—plan, act, and reflect—they are the cornerstones of a good flight and of a good business. You need to build routines into your business from beginning to end. Before we start the engines, let me explain.

"Some people are great action-takers and movers. However, we want to know that what we are doing is what needs to be done. That is why creating routines around planning is important. Planning is the art of charting a course, setting clear objectives, and envisioning a desired future. It is a deliberate act of envisioning where we align our actions with our aspirations.

"We're about to plan our way onto the runway and into the air, and if we don't plan, we're not going to make it very far into the air. Even if we do, we'll still get lost up there and we may never find this runway again. In fact, before I even take flight, I give my flight plan to the tower." Ray pointed to the air traffic control tower. "The air traffic controllers are part of my team as well, and they need to know my plan."

"I get it, Ray—we need to create routine planning activities into our work," Scott said.

Ray nodded and gave a thumbs-up. "It also helps you avoid needless or hapless mistakes. The more intentional you are about making planning a routine, the more clarity you will have on every journey.

"Taking action," Ray continued, "is the next step beyond planning. It's the moment when we take that first step, where we execute our plans with unwavering commitment. Action brings ideas to life, propelling us toward our goals. You can plan all day long, but if you don't take action, your plans won't lift off anymore than we will today. I plan to take flight soon, Scott, but if I don't start taking action right here in this cockpit, we'll just sit here on the ground forever."

Scott chuckled. "Well, I certainly don't want to stay on the ground, Ray, so let's take action and fly!"

Ray laughed again and said, "Not quite, Scott— one more step—but don't forget that your actions need routines as well. Your actions will either lift you up toward your goal or pull you down toward a crash. All actions take you either up or down; there's no in-between."

Ray also explained that routines are not synonymous with actions. "For example," he continued, "when you are taking action or going through your activities—working out your plan—there might be regular routines that are sabotaging the effort. For example, your estimating department might not deliver drawings or estimates to the operations department because the department directors don't like each other. It's not an SOP, but it is a routine that is hurting the overall mission and vision of the company."

"I get it," replied Scott.

Ray proceeded. "Finally, Scott, planning and acting routines without reflection is like the blind flying the blind. Reflection routines allow us to pause, assess our progress, and to learn from our experiences. It's the key that unlocks insights, enabling us to refine our approach and adapt to the ever-changing skies. You'll see what I mean when we lift off. Watch how I'll routinely review and reflect on my charts, the gauges, and navigational instruments, ensuring alignment with the intended route."

"Will do, Ray." Scott realized that reflection is not a passive act but an active one—a catalyst for growth, enabling him to learn from both triumphs and setbacks and to course-correct along the way. He also realized that every team needs built-in reflection routines.

Ray finally leaned back, his eyes fixed on the horizon. "Scott," he said as he turned on the engine and his voice carrying the weight of conviction, "the beauty lies in the integration of these three types of routines. Planning without action is mere wishful thinking, action without reflection is a missed opportunity for growth, and reflection without planning is a cycle of stagnation. Together, they form progress. But without good routines, you can't propel your team toward greatness."

Scott's spirit soared as the engine roared, his mind ablaze with newfound understanding, propelling him ever closer to his aspirations as a leader.

"Now, Scott," Ray said, his voice infused with confidence and authority, "let me show you how to fly!" Scott's eyes widened with a mixture of excitement and trepidation. The runway stretched out before him like a ribbon of possibility. With Ray's guidance, he felt a surge of confidence, knowing that he was in capable hands.

Ray established communication with the tower before doing the pre-taxi check. He tested the radio to ensure it crackled to life with the familiar voices of the control tower. "Now we need to plan our pre-taxi check. This involves verifying that the flight controls respond correctly and that our navigation instruments are aligned."

Scott followed Ray's lead, his hands moving across the control yoke and pedals. He marveled at the precision with which Ray manipulated the controls, instilling a sense of reverence for the mastery of flight. With the pre-taxi plan complete, Ray instructed Scott on the art of taxiing. Together, they took action and maneuvered the aircraft, weaving their way through the taxiways. Scott listened attentively to Ray's guidance, learning to navigate the both steering and braking, ensuring their safe passage to the runway.

As they approached the runway, Ray's voice took on a deeper tone. "Scott, that runway is the threshold of our dreams. It represents the moment when we leave the ground and embrace the freedom of the skies."

Scott's heart swelled with emotion. He understood the significance of this moment, the culmination of countless hours of restoration. Then Ray guided Scott through the process of aligning the aircraft with the runway, ensuring their trajectory was accurate. He explained the routine of checking on the proper power settings and smoothly engaging the throttle to propel them forward. Scott's hands trembled with anticipation as he followed Ray's lead, feeling the aircraft respond to his touch as he took action.

With Ray's encouragement, Scott pushed the throttle forward, feeling the surge of power as the aircraft surged down the runway. The world around them blurred, as if time itself could not keep pace with their momentum. As they hurtled down the runway, the wind rushing through their hair, Scott couldn't help but laugh. He glanced at Ray, their eyes meeting in a silent acknowledgment of their shared triumph. Ray saluted Scott.

Scott felt a real sense of awe as the aircraft gracefully lifted of the ground. In a dance between the heavens and the earth, as they soared through the skies, Scott grasped the importance of the gauges in the airplane cockpit. He and Ray scanned the instrument panel, observing the readings that provided insights into the aircraft's performance. Each gauge held a story—a narrative of the engine's health, the altitude, the airspeed, and more. Scott recognized that viewing the gauges enabled him to assess the aircraft's condition, make informed decisions, and ensure the safety of the flight. It was through this constant observation that he could identify potential issues, adjust course as needed, and maintain equilibrium between the machine and the elements. In the cockpit's array of gauges, Scott discovered why understanding the nuanced readings facilitated the navigation of the skies with confidence.

With each passing moment, he and Ray monitored the altitude, airspeed, and fuel consumption. Scott understood how assessing the flight plan in real time allowed him to adapt to changing conditions, navigate unforeseen challenges, and optimize the journey toward their destination. It was a dance between preparation and adaptability, a delicate balance that ensured they stayed in flight. Through this ongoing assessment, Scott realized the power of routine decision-making, where clarity and situational awareness merged to guide them toward a successful flight. Ray's routines guided the way, and nothing was left to chance.

As the aircraft soared higher, leaving the earth behind, their spirits were liberated. With the wind on their faces, together they witnessed the dance of sunlight on clouds, the breathtaking vistas that unfolded beneath their two wings. Ray and Scott forged an unbreakable bond that day—a connection forged by their shared love of flight. The blue skies became their sanctuary where dreams took flight and the boundaries of human achievement were defied. They flew for hours, and then Ray began to prepare to guide Scott through the art of landing an airplane.

But during the flight, Scott thought about what it meant to be an effective team leader. If he was going to take his team to new heights, he'd have to learn how to harness the power of routines. Building a good team was about more than finding purpose, creating expectations and accountability, and keeping things simple. It was also about creating routines so they would follow through and finish what they started. Routines are the engine that produces purposeful results that stabilize teams.

Then Ray motioned to Scott to look down, where Scott noticed a small leather notebook on the floor of the cockpit, pen attached. It was embossed with the words "Scott's Routines." Scott smiled and opened the notebook, hurriedly taking these notes:

Routines are our stable and consistent daily activities. By intentionally designing predictable patterns, routines create a sense of order and structure, helping individuals and teams to better manage uncertainty and navigate with greater confidence.

Routines streamline processes and reduce decision fatigue. When tasks become routine, they require less mental effort, allowing individuals and teams to focus on more critical aspects of their work. This efficiency maximizes productivity and ensures resources are utilized effectively.

Routines establish predictable environments for team members to work together efficiently. Knowing what to expect and how to interact with colleagues fosters a culture of trust. This fosters a sense of camaraderie, leading to stronger team dynamics and increased collaboration.

Routines can either be uplifting or detrimental. Don't assume that all routines are good; in fact, many people and teams are stuck in some destructive routines. Once you identify the bad routines and replace them with good ones, you'll experience transformation. By continually evaluating the effect of routines, individuals and teams can ensure that they are being propelled forward rather than held back, striking a balance that maintains growth and vitality.

Scott was still thinking and writing when Ray's voice interrupted. "Scott, let me show you how to land the airplane with grace and precision, bringing it safely back to the earth. Once again, we need to stick to our routines. We need to plan, act, and reflect, and as always, stick to our routines."

Scott's eyes flickered with a mix of anticipation and respect. Landing an airplane was more than a technical skill; it was a culmination of experience, judgment, and the fine-tuning of instincts. With

Ray by his side, Scott felt he was ready for this crucial aspect of flight.

"First," Ray instructed, "we must plan a stable approach, the foundation of a successful landing, maintaining a steady airspeed and descent rate, making subtle adjustments as needed to align with the runway." Scott observed Ray's precise movements, his keen eye monitoring the instrument panel, ensuring their approach remained steady. "Next," Ray continued, "we must manage our flaps and landing gear. Gradually deploy the flaps to increase lift and reduce airspeed to ensure the landing gear is fully extended, ready to cushion our return to the earth." Scott mirrored Ray's actions, the aircraft responding to his touch. He felt the subtle shifts in control, the harmonious dance between man and machine that ensured a controlled descent.

Ray's voice carried a gentle urgency as he explained the art of flare—the crucial moment when the aircraft nears the runway. "Scott, as we approach the runway threshold, we must reduce our descent rate and gradually level the airplane. It's vital to focus on the instrument panel. Trust the instruments and feel the energy of the aircraft as it transitions from flight to landing. Remember we can trust the instruments because we stuck to the routines. We know they'll work correctly because we made sure of it beforehand."

Scott's heart raced. He watched Ray's expert hands, mirroring the subtle adjustments, his instincts aligning with the shared rhythm of their movements. As the wheels neared the ground, Scott listened intently to Ray's guidance on the art of touching down. "Scott, ease back on the controls, allowing the aircraft to settle gently onto the runway. Keep a light touch, but maintain control as we decelerate."

In that fleeting moment, Scott felt the weight of responsibility, the delicate balance between control and surrender. With Ray's voice guiding him, he executed the touchdown with finesse, feeling the wheels connect with the earth like a dancer's final step. The runway stretched out before them, a symbol of their triumph. They rolled down the runway and the aircraft slowed to a halt. The flight was safe and successful, and the world outside seemed to hold its breath, recognizing the significance of their safe return.

With the airplane safely on the ground, Scott basked in the euphoria of achievement. The landing was not just a technical maneuver; it was also the culmination of his dreams to fly a small plane. Through Ray's mentorship, he had unlocked the artistry of landing, merging his dreams with actions.

As they taxied to the hangar, Scott understood that landing was not just about returning to the earth but also about embracing the importance of routines. With Ray as his guide, he had embarked on a journey that extended far beyond the runway—it was a journey he hoped to also master as an effective team leader.

As they walked back to the hangar, Ray said, "Remember, Scott, the dance of a good routine is needed every step of the way, when planning, acting, and reflecting, and it's not just a one-time performance—it is a lifelong commitment. Embrace it, refine it, and they will help your team align."

Scott understood that this dance was not just a means to an end, but rather a blueprint for good teamwork. While dreaming a big dream and casting a big vision is a start, the real essence of the achievement is in the mundane.

"Routines provide structure and consistency, and they demonstrate that we have alignment of actions with vision."

13

Scott Returns to the Office

Scott's return to the bustling office marked a pivotal moment. Armed with Ray's wisdom, he was determined to share the impact of building routines with his team.

As the team settled into their seats for the Monday morning meeting, Scott told everyone about his flight with Ray. It was enjoyable as he shared everything with the group. Since all the team members worked in aviation, they bonded once again as they listened to Scott's flight story. Then he launched into his message on routines. Scott's voice resonated with purpose as he addressed the team, repeating what Ray told him and describing what he experienced in the skies.

"Routines are the building blocks of success," Scott began. "Over the past weeks and months, we've worked hard to come together as a team, and we've made amazing progress. But until we learn how to build effective routines into our workdays, and get rid of the routines that are holding us back, we might never reach the goals we've set for ourselves. Routines provide structure and consistency, and they demonstrate that we have an alignment of our actions with our vision and values. By integrating intentional habits into our work, we can drive and more effectively manage our productivity, foster better collaboration, and propel us toward our goals."

With imagery from his time in the air, Scott painted a picture of how routines could shape their daily work, foster a culture of continuous improvement, and amplify their collective impact.

He also explained his desire to cultivate a culture that prioritized the growth of its individuals. This realization prompted him to announce a regular practice that could foster trust, facilitate feedback, and bolster communication between managers and their respective team members. So starting the following week, the company would begin individualized one-on-one sessions with managers and their team members. And Scott didn't run this by Gary; he established one-on-one meetings company-wide on his own.

He also took his team on a deep dive into planning, acting, and regular reflection—an opportunity to learn from both successes and setbacks, to adapt their approach, and to continually refine their work together. As Scott unveiled this vision of a routine-driven workplace with one-on-one meetings, another incredible transformation began to unfold. Routines were no longer perceived as mundane tasks but rather as catalysts for collective success—an avenue to channel their efforts, align their purpose, and propel them closer to their goals. The team eagerly embraced Scott's call to action. The members committed themselves to integrating routines into their work, recognizing that excellence was not an isolated event but a series of deliberate habits interwoven into all of their work.

In the days and weeks that followed, the team developed a series of routines based on their plans, actions, and reflections. The associates wholeheartedly embraced Scott's routine one-on-one meetings, cultivating a culture of trust and collaboration. Once these energizing routines were implemented, the power of regular reflection was harnessed, allowing them to seize opportunities for growth and embrace the continuous improvement process.

Gary first caught wind of the one-on-one meetings and responded with skepticism, dismissing them as another potential time sink. However, as time went on, he couldn't help but notice a curious trend. Across the company, fewer mistakes were being made, and processes seemed smoother than before. While he never openly expressed gratitude to Scott for spearheading the implementation of these meetings, he also refrained from obstructing them. This unspoken acknowledgment spoke volumes— Gary's initial skepticism had transformed into a silent recognition of the value these interactions were adding to the organization.

One evening, when Scott and Sarah were home chatting after dinner, she couldn't help but chuckle softly. It seemed that the tide was turning, and even the most skeptical were starting to see the positive changes Scott had initiated. With a playful grin, she reminded him of the time she had affectionately dubbed him a "rock star" and predicted his ability to orchestrate a turnaround. Sarah playfully nudged him, recounting how she had also mused about him meeting someone who would become instrumental in his journey. As she reflected on these moments, a mischievous glint sparkled in her eyes. "You know," she mused, "I think it would be quite interesting for me to meet your friend Ray someday."

SECTION 4

Rituals

"Camaraderie, anticipation, and a sense of purpose are the keys to revitalizing momentum."

14

The Airshow

The next morning, Scott had an idea. While he drank his coffee, he suggested to Sarah that they go to the airfield for an air show the following day. She happily said yes, mentioning how she was looking forward to seeing the airplane that had been restored. But what got her even more excited was the chance to finally meet Ray. "I've heard so much about him from you. I'm actually excited to finally meet him. It's like meeting a mystery person I've only heard stories about!"

So Scott and Sarah searched for Ray the next morning, hoping to find him at the hangar or nearby. To their surprise, he was nowhere to be found. However, Scott found a note affixed to the airplane. The words scrawled on it revealed that Ray had left to run some errands. Intrigued by the bustling activity and increased footfall at the airport, they made their way to the terminal to check out the commotion, where they were greeted by a sea of people, their eyes all turned skyward, witnessing the captivating sight of airplanes taking off and landing.

It was an air show unlike any Scott had ever experienced. The crowd's enthusiasm reminded him of what he'd encountered at NCAA football games with his sons. He soon discovered that air shows were cherished traditions, interweaving a rich tapestry of customs that elevated the entire experience, cementing a deep aviation culture. Scott and his wife marveled at the way these time-honored rituals had become ingrained in the very essence of air shows, creating a collective sense of anticipation, camaraderie, and pride among all who participated.

As with every air show, this one commenced with a grand opening ceremony, which set the stage for the extraordinary spectacle to come. With the resonating strains of the National Anthem, fluttering flags proudly presented, and inspiring speeches evoking a shared passion for flight, the ceremony ignited a collective spirit of excitement and anticipation. When everyone stood and sang the National Anthem together, Scott shed a tear and beamed with pride.

As the show continued, it wasn't just an airplane flying overhead. Anyone could see that any day at any airport. Instead, the skies had become a canvas for precision and artistry. Flyovers, executed by military aircraft or skilled demonstration teams, displayed amazing aerial maneuvers and formations. Among them, the missing man formations stood out, a poignant tribute to fallen aviators. In a solemn ritual, one aircraft departed from a formation, symbolizing the absence of a comrade who had made the ultimate sacrifice. Scott saluted the skies along with the crowd.

Then a series of aerobatic displays took center stage, dazzling spectators with astonishing aerial feats. Skilled pilots commanded their aircraft to defy gravity, executing loops, rolls, spins, dives, and other mesmerizing maneuvers. Each choreographed routine was a testament to the mastery of the pilot and the boundless capabilities of his flying machine. The audience was spellbound, and Scott's heart raced in synchrony with the engines that roared above.

The air show also embraced the daring world of wing walking and skydiving. Fearless performers stood on the wings of moving aircraft, showcasing awe-inspiring acrobatics that defied all conventional limits. Meanwhile, parachutists descended from the heavens, their graceful freefalls punctuated by precision landings, demonstrating the artistry of human flight.

The excitement wasn't only in the sky. On the ground, the show offered more than mere aerial spectacles. Attendees were also treated to a display of static aircraft exhibits, a chance to immerse themselves in the world of aviation. Up close, they could explore the intricate details of various aircraft, engage with pilots, and expand their knowledge of the vast array of flying machines. This ritual of exploration bridged the gap between aviation enthusiasts and the wider public, nurturing their fascination with flight. Scott and Sarah spent time visiting with pilots, and they also kept a lookout for Ray, who was still missing. "I'm surprised Ray isn't here," Scott said.

After lunch, Scott saw how a profound appreciation for the armed forces is deeply rooted in an air show. Military tributes paid homage to the brave men and women who serve or have served in defense of our nation. Through a military band, honor guard, color guard, and ceremonial rituals, the air show honored their sacrifices and contributions, fostering a deep sense of gratitude and respect. Scott and Sarah shared memories of his uncle Steve, who served as a pilot in Afghanistan.

In the culmination of the air show, a grand ceremony unfolded, honoring the best of the best within the aviation community. The atmosphere was electric as pilots, aircraft crews, and organizations took center stage to receive recognition for their extraordinary achievements and significant contributions to the world of aviation. This prestigious award ceremony, a symbol of excellence and innovation, served not only as a tribute to their accomplishments but also as a catalyst to inspire and propel future advancements in the field. But still no Ray. Surely he was here somewhere.

As the ceremony drew to a close, a sense of anticipation filled the air. All eyes turned toward the runway, where a lone biplane stood poised for an unexpected finale. Scott and Sarah, in the midst of the crowd, couldn't quite comprehend the buzz surrounding a distant biplane. Nonetheless, the enthusiasm of the spectators remained unabated, their cheers reverberating through the air. With a burst of energy, the biplane roared down the runway, soaring into the sky. At first, Scott couldn't fathom what set this flight apart, but he then realized it was the same plane he helped to restore, and Ray was the pilot! The crowd's exuberance persisted as the plane gracefully maneuvered above, tracing patterns against the azure canvas. Several laps later, it descended for a landing, its approach slow and deliberate.

As Ray and his plane drew near, a resounding cannon blast punctuated the end of the event. The atmosphere crackled with anticipation as the crowd surged forward, eager to witness the climax of this remarkable display. And then, something unexpected unfolded before Scott's eyes. Throngs of people surrounded the plane, and as Ray climbed out, they walked triumphantly with him toward the hangar. The significance of the moment was not lost on Scott. Amidst the jubilant chaos, Ray's eyes briefly met his, and in that fleeting exchange, a grin broke across his face as he saluted Scott, a gesture reciprocated with heartfelt reverence. Ray walked over, and they shook hands. "Can't talk now, Scott, but I'll see you tomorrow! And it's nice to meet you, Mrs.!" he smiled and exclaimed and he turned to Sarah. Then, as if swept away by the sea of enthusiasts, he disappeared into the crowd.

Scott was caught in a bittersweet reverie as the crowd slowly dispersed. In that fleeting encounter, he had glimpsed a profound truth—a reminder of the impact that ritual can have on a community, an industry, or even a single life. The day's events had ignited a spirit of celebration and unity, leaving an indelible mark on all those who bore witness.

As Scott absorbed the vibrant atmosphere around him, he couldn't help but feel a renewed sense of energy and inspiration. The rituals and customs of the air show, with their profound impact on both participants and spectators, captivated his senses and stirred something within him. It was as if the very fabric of aviation had come alive before his eyes, reminding him of the potential for greatness that lay dormant within his team.

With the air show as his backdrop, Scott found himself contemplating how these rituals could be adapted and integrated into his own office environment. The camaraderie, anticipation, and sense of purpose that permeated the air show held the key to revitalizing his team's momentum. As the planes soared overhead, Scott's mind brimmed with ideas and possibilities, envisioning a workplace where rituals could ignite passion, foster connection, and fuel the pursuit of excellence.

Inspired and invigorated, he resolved to seek Ray's wisdom upon his return, knowing that the insights gleaned from the world of aviation would breathe new life into their work and reignite the spark that had momentarily waned. He could hardly wait to find Ray the next day and talk to him about rituals.

Scott and Sarah talked all evening about the air show. They enjoyed it and their time together. "You know," she said, "I really hope we get to know Ray better some day. He seems like the kind of person with stories to tell and wisdom to share."

"Indeed, he's been a great friend and mentor to me," Scott answered. "It would be nice for you to get to know him better, too. I'll see if we can all have dinner soon."

"Rituals are a catalyst for appreciation, contemplation, and a reminder to savor the present moment."

15

Scott's New Rituals

The following morning, Scott arrived at the office bright and early, his steps purposeful as walked briskly to locate Ray and his airplane. Intrigued by the fervent cheers and applause Ray had received the previous day, along with his prominent role in the grand finale flyover, Scott's curiosity burned bright. What was it about his friend that had elicited such exuberance from the crowd? And why had he been chosen for the pivotal closing act?

Upon reaching the airplane, Scott discovered Ray in a deep slumber, comfortably seated in his chair with his head tipped toward his chest. Scott silently observed him for a few moments until a resounding snore broke the tranquility, startling the pilot awake. His initial bewilderment quickly transformed into laughter, and he sat up, greeting Scott with a warm smile.

"Well, hello there, Scott," Ray chuckled. "Did you enjoy the show yesterday?"

Scott's face lit up with enthusiasm as he recalled the spectacle of the air show. "I sure did, Ray!" he exclaimed. "But I can't help but wonder, how did you end up closing the ceremonies?"

Ray, still enveloped in amusement, replied, "Must be my goggles." His laughter filled the air, but he offered no further explanation. Instead, he turned the conversation toward Scott. "Did you glean any insights from the show that might prove helpful in your office?"

"Absolutely," he responded. "The air show reminded me of the power of rituals and the sense of camaraderie they evoke. It made me realize that we need to inject some meaning and engagement into our workplace. And that's where I could use your guidance, Ray."

Ray's eyes sparkled with a mix of wisdom and mischief. He was aware that this was the moment Scott had been waiting for—the opportunity to learn from the unique experiences and perspectives of the aviation world. "Ask away, Scott," Ray encouraged, ready to share his knowledge.

Scott took a deep breath, his mind teeming with questions, eager to tap into Ray's wellspring of insights. This was an opportunity to bridge the gap between the thrill of the air show and the dynamics of his office. And so, with curiosity and determination, Scott began to ask his questions, knowing that Ray's wisdom would illuminate a path forward, infusing his workplace with the vitality and inspiration he had witnessed soaring high above.

As they delved into conversation, Scott felt a surge of anticipation. Ray's presence, like an aviation maestro, held the promise of unlocking hidden potential, propelling his team toward new heights. In that moment, they walked into the hangar together, and Ray started writing on the whiteboard.

"Scott, rituals are more than mere routines or reminders," Ray began, his voice filled with conviction. "Rituals are intrinsic to our human nature. When we participate in religious ceremonies, celebrate birthdays, or gather for a Thanksgiving feast, we engage in rituals. These moments allow us to pause the relentless pace of life and be fully present, appreciating the significance of the occasion. Rituals are a catalyst for appreciation, contemplation, and a reminder to savor the present moment. They connect us to something bigger than ourselves."

As Ray continued, his words resonated with Scott, painting a vivid picture of the power of rituals in the workplace. Ray emphasized the importance of rituals in nurturing a strong company culture and instilling a sense of belonging within the organization. "When leaders embrace and ritualize certain experiences, they mitigate the risk of work becoming an endless grind. Instead, rituals infuse meaning into the everyday and contribute to a vibrant and engaged workforce."

To illustrate his point, Ray walked over to the whiteboard and began jotting down four significant reasons why rituals are vital in the workplace:

- **Promotion:** "This is when an organization wants to promote certain behaviors, for example, ringing a bell in the office if you close a sale over a certain amount. This ritual reinforces positive behaviors and encourages others to strive for similar achievements."

- **Acceptance:** "This is when a group of people wants to show that someone is now accepted into the group. Doctors give out white coats, Air Force pilots give out wings, and all companies can have a signing day. These rituals symbolize inclusion and foster a sense of belonging."

- **Significance:** "This is when an organization makes sure certain ideas remain significant, for example, giving stickers out to place on hard hats to identify core values on a project. Such rituals reinforce the importance of the organization's values and encourage employees to uphold them."

- **Transitions:** "Whenever there is a transition such retirement, marriage, birth, graduation, or promotion, traditions are a great way to honor the individuals and their accomplishments. These rituals acknowledge change and celebrate milestones, reinforcing a sense of achievement and progress."

Ray emphasized that these rituals serve multiple purposes—they build community by allowing individuals to partake in shared experiences; increase engagement by promoting employee motivation, productivity, and job satisfaction; encourage teamwork and collaboration by providing opportunities for interaction and cooperation; celebrate achievements and milestones by acknowledging hard work and contributions; facilitate organizational change by providing a familiar framework during transitions; and reinforce values and company culture by continually reminding employees of what the organization stands for.

With these lessons etched in his mind, Scott eagerly sought to apply them within his own organization. He knew that embracing rituals would not only reinforce their values and sense of community, but would also infuse their work with purpose and meaning. With Ray's guidance, Scott felt empowered to transform his workplace into a hub of inspiration, connection, and fulfillment. Drawing inspiration from the captivating air show, a spectacle that held particular significance for his aviation-oriented team, Scott set out to infuse the work environment with a sense of awe and inspiration. Serendipitously, he discovered that a few of his team members had also attended the air show, providing a valuable opportunity for collaboration in shaping these rituals.

As the weeks unfolded, Scott eagerly announced a new ritual influenced by the awe-inspiring tradition of flyovers at air shows and other significant events, a tradition that conveys respect and admiration to those being honored. He called the new ritual "Fly Over." This aimed to celebrate and acknowledge employees who showcased exceptional dedication and consistently exceeded expectations. During quarterly mini-meetings in smaller groups, and then at a company-wide end-of-year banquet, Scott's team would be celebrated. Fly Over promised to be a ritual that would last for years and would be embedded in the team's culture.

For the first annual banquet, which was held soon after the air show, Dave's wife took the stage to share a heartfelt story about her late husband, explaining the significance of the company and the importance of the award. She also discussed the company's core values before sharing a tale about the nominated individual, ultimately revealing the Employee of the Year. This individual then joined her on stage to receive a special photograph, signed on the mat by all employees and framed with reclaimed airplane aluminum—a material reflecting Dave's passion for connection. Following the presentation, the entire staff stood and formed two lines, creating a tunnel from the stage. As the honoree ran through the tunnel, the employees all extended their hands for high-fives and cheered enthusiastically, symbolically "flying over" the recipient to recognize the employee's commitment to the company's values.

Prior to the banquet, Gary didn't hold back in sharing his discontent with Scott and the other managers, firmly asserting his belief that the banquet was an unnecessary and extravagant use of funds. His dissatisfaction was evident, and he made his opinion known. In fact, when the banquet commenced, Gary's mood seemed unchanged as he chose a seat toward the back. Throughout the event, his demeanor remained visibly sullen, reflecting his ongoing disapproval and reluctance to embrace the festivities. He left early.

As Scott diligently implemented rituals, their impact on the team became palpable. The air show–inspired traditions served as catalysts, fostering an environment where passion, camaraderie, and motivation thrived. Through them, Scott successfully instilled a sense of awe, celebration, and genuine appreciation among his team members. Inspired by the extraordinary world of aviation, these rituals took flight, transforming their workplace into a realm where miracles were celebrated, wings were earned, and the spirit of teamwork soared to new heights.

Scott was admittedly surprised by the impact the new rituals had on his team. He truly didn't expect how they reverberated through every aspect of the company. One of the most significant changes was the boost in team morale and job satisfaction. The rituals Scott introduced not only provided a sense of stability and predictability, but they also fostered a deeper sense of connection among team members. Over time, the rituals became ingrained in the team's culture. Celebrating small wins and acknowledging individual contributions further fueled motivation and enthusiasm. The team began to take ownership of the rituals, suggesting improvements and adaptations that suited their evolving needs.

As productivity increased due to better organization and improved communication, the team started achieving their goals more consistently. This success, in turn, fueled a positive feedback loop! Accomplishments were celebrated, boosting morale even further and solidifying the connection between rituals, productivity, and job satisfaction.

Scott had transformed into a self-assured leader who had mastered the art of crafting a company culture that placed a premium on its workforce. He had come to grasp the significance of nurturing an environment where individuals felt valued, their opinions were sought after, and their purposes were encouraged. He had honed the ability to consistently guide his team, reinforcing the hows, whys, and whats of their roles. The cornerstone of this evolved culture was his one-on-one meetings, which had evolved from a mere practice into the very heart of the company's ethos.

Scott credited Ray with his transformation and the company's survival, and he'd make weekly trips to the airport hangar where his mentor remained between flights. But Ray was always quiet when asked about his background and experience.

"There's power in three
simple leadership principles:
reminders, routines,
and rituals."

16

Lift!

One morning, Gary stepped into Scott's office, his face filled with bewilderment. "I've been let go," he declared, his words devoid of emotion. Taking a seat across from Scott's desk, he fell silent, fixating his gaze on the ceiling above. After a prolonged pause, he uttered, "Congratulations, Scott." Shaking his head in disbelief, Gary rose from his chair and departed the office, leaving Scott perplexed and yearning for answers.

At a loss as to the meaning behind Gary's cryptic words, Scott rose from his seat and began pacing the office in search of clarity. Everything appeared to be business as usual. The diligent hum of coworkers engrossed in their tasks filled the air, with no apparent signs of disruption. Driven by curiosity, he decided to take a breather and seek out Ray, hoping to find some insight. However, much to his surprise, his friend was nowhere to be found. The hangar, typically Ray's sanctuary, stood empty, devoid of its usual activity. Scott retraced his steps back to the office.

Upon his return, an unexpected scene unfolded before him—a small group of coworkers was gathered around Ray in lively conversation. But this was not the same Ray he knew, the one who wore threadbare jeans as he toiled away on his aircraft. Instead, he was transformed, impeccably groomed, clad in a classic business suit. Scott was completely confused. Why was he in the conference room?

Ray approached Scott, extending a hand for a firm shake. They exchanged greetings, and in the midst of his lingering confusion, Scott mustered the courage to ask, "Ray, what brings you here?"

With a gracious smile, Ray proposed, "Let's adjourn to your office, Scott."

They walked side by side, Scott's mind still swimming with bewilderment, until they both settled into his office.

"Scott, my name is Ray Rutherford," he began, shedding light on his true identity. "When I'm not tinkering with that old plane, I specialize in fixing companies."

It suddenly dawned on Scott who Ray truly was—a legendary figure in the aviation community, a revered entrepreneur, a CEO extraordinaire, and a renowned builder within the industry: Ray Rutherford, the Steve Jobs of aviation.

Ray continued speaking, although Scott's focus wavered, struggling to fully comprehend the momentous conversation. However, one phrase finally pierced through his muddled thoughts: "Scott, I've acquired the company, and I want you to be my CEO." That message hit him with tremendous force, leaving him momentarily speechless. He, Scott, was to be the CEO of the company!

Overwhelmed with gratitude, Scott stammered, "Ray, I can't express my appreciation enough."

Ray, ever humble, responded, "No need to thank me, Scott. You did the hard work, not me."

Scott interjected, recognizing Ray's pivotal role. "That may not be entirely true. Your guidance, your words—Ray, you made a difference."

Ray chuckled warmly, replying, "I simply provided the guidance, Scott. The rest was your doing. But you know what? Let's take a stroll."

Standing up, Ray motioned for Scott to follow as they ventured out of the office and away from the building. They strode along a familiar path, leading to the aging airplane that had long been Scott's refuge. Yet, in that moment, it no longer appeared weathered and worn. Instead, it radiated a newfound brilliance, shimmering under the sunlight. Ray hopped into the cockpit, beckoning Scott to join him. They donned their goggles.

"Come on, Scott. Let's soar into the wild blue yonder," Ray declared. Eagerly, Scott took his place beside him. The engine roared to life, and Ray meticulously completed the preflight preparations. In no time, the aircraft hurtled down the runway, defying gravity as it gracefully ascended into the sky. A wave of exhilaration swept over Scott, and as the plane soared above the building that housed his workplace, he realized the invaluable lessons Ray had imparted to him. It was a moment of profound self-discovery, a testament to how far he had come.

Under Ray's tutelage, Scott had learned the power of simple yet effective leadership principles— reminders, routines, and rituals—that had transformed not only the team but also his own life. He was no longer the same person he had been. Ray's teachings had equipped him with the tools to achieve lift-off, propelling him toward a future that brimmed with promise. With the azure sky stretching before them, Scott and Ray laughed together, basking in the splendor of the present moment. "Lift-off!" Ray proclaimed jubilantly. As their aircraft traversed the vast expanse, Scott's heart swelled with gratitude, knowing that his trajectory had forever been altered by the wisdom of a true visionary.

As the new CEO, Scott led his team and the entire company to new heights and to becoming the industry leader in airplane parts. As for Ray, he continued to tinker with old airplanes, checking in with Scott every so often, and enjoying an occasional dinner with both him and Sarah.

Resources

1on1's Coaching System: Are you looking to increase coaching and development on your team or organization? Try our new 1on1's Coaching System App. Learn more about it at www.ThinkMoveThrive. com/1on1-app/

Other Books from ThinkMoveThrive: Check out MOVE! If you are in a transition period in life or going through a "Now what?" moment then MOVE! was written for you.

The Last 10%: Listen to Dallas host a podcast designed to help inspire, equip, and encourage leaders/coaches in organizations to finish well and finish strong. Guests range from mental performance coaches, to former professional athletes, to business leaders and everything in between. You can find it on all major podcast platforms by searching The Last 10% or on our website.

Take the Enneagram Assessment! Try our Enneagram Assessment. The report is free for a limited time. You can find it on our website at https://www. ThinkMoveThrive.com/enneagram-assessment/

www.ingramcontent.com/pod-product-compliance
Lightning Source LLC
Chambersburg PA
CBHW021929190326
41519CB00009B/965